Re-focus on
Child Abuse

Re-focus on
Child Abuse

Medical, Legal and
Social Work Perspectives

Edited by Allan Levy QC

HAWKSMERE

© 1994 Hawksmere plc

Published by:
Hawksmere plc
12–18 Grosvenor Gardens
Belgravia
London SW1 0DH

ISBN 1 85418 041 X

A CIP catalogue record for this book is available from the British Library.

Editorial and production in association with
Book Production Consultants plc, Cambridge.

Typeset by KeyStar, St Ives, Cambridgeshire.

Printed at Alden Press Limited, Oxford and Northampton, Great Britain

CONTENTS

...children are especially vulnerable. They have not formed the defences inside themselves which older people have, and, therefore, need especial protection. They are also a country's most valuable asset for the future.

Mr Justice Latey, *Re X* [1975] Fam 47, at 52

EDITOR

Allan Levy QC chaired the Pindown Inquiry in Staffordshire and has written, broadcast and lectured extensively on child law.

CONTRIBUTORS

Dr Frank Bamford is a consultant paediatrician.

Margery Bray is a social work consultant.

Dame Elizabeth Butler-Sloss is a Court of Appeal judge.

Dr Peter Dean is a forensic medical examiner and HM Coroner (Essex No.2 District).

John Ellison is a solicitor in private practice.

Professor M. D. A. Freeman is Professor of English Law at University College, London.

Susan Hall is a detective inspector, Northumbria Police.

Michael Hinchliffe is a senior solicitor in the Official Solicitor's Office.

Barbara Joel-Esam is a solicitor with the NSPCC.

Michael Lawson QC is a barrister specialising in criminal law.

Professor Roy Meadow is Professor of Paediatrics and Child Health, St James's University Hospital, Leeds.

Peter Newell is Coordinator of EPOCH (End Physical Punishment of Children).

Philippa Russell is Director of the Council for Disabled Children.

Peter Smith is a guardian ad litem and a social services inspector.

Dr Stephen Wolkind is a consultant psychiatrist, Maudsley Hospital.

INTRODUCTION

Allan Levy QC

Focus on Child Abuse was published in 1989.[1] It appears that it was widely read and referred to, and this book has been produced as a follow-up volume after a gap of five years.

Since 1989 there have been many momentous events. A roll-call of inquiries includes Orkney,[2] Pindown in Staffordshire,[3] and Leicestershire:[4] a depressing catalogue of man's (and woman's) inhumanity to children. It is not an exaggeration to observe that a child in care in the 1990s may well be a child in danger.

Lord Clyde's Orkney Report in 1992 could be described as Cleveland[5] revisited. It contained the same condemnation of the too hasty removal of children from their homes, the failure to treat children as individuals, the poor interviewing and the lack of inter-agency consultation and coordination. It seemed as if few lessons had been learned. The judgment in the Rochdale case[6] also revealed the same despairing picture in relation to much-publicised and inaccurate allegations of so-called satanic or ritual abuse.

Two major events, one international and the other national, however, provide some inspiration and a qualified optimism. In December 1991 the United Kingdom ratified the United Nations Convention on the Rights of the Child.[7] Article 19 of the Convention states that:

> 1. State Parties shall take all appropriate legislative, administrative, social and educational measures to protect the child from all forms of physical or mental violence, injury or abuse, neglect or negligent treatment, maltreatment or exploitation including sexual abuse, while in the care of parents, legal guardians or any other person who has the care of the child.

> 2. Such protective measures should, as appropriate, include effective procedures for the establishment of social programmes to provide necessary support for the child and for those who have the care of the child, as well as for other forms of prevention and for identification, reporting, referral, investigation, treatment, and follow-up of instances of child maltreatment described heretofore, and, as appropriate, for judicial involvement.

The UN Convention is an important measure in itself as well as being a yardstick by which domestic activity may be tested. In England and Wales (and with limited effect in Scotland and Northern Ireland), the Children Act 1989, a major reforming statute, was implemented in October 1991, and aims to simplify, to reform, to coordinate, to integrate and to make the courts more user-friendly. It is far too early to evaluate its effect but it is a genuine attempt to streamline the law within a framework that tries to balance the often competing interests of the child, the parent and the state, and to provide practical and effective measures in the field of child protection.

Certain aspects of child protection continue to need urgent attention. The investigative stage regarding alleged child abuse, particularly the interviewing of children, for example, requires to be continually under the microscope. The plight of the child witness in criminal proceedings still needs much attention. Consideration of the interaction between civil and criminal proceedings in which a child is involved is in its infancy. Expert medical and social work evidence relating to many aspects of child protection gives rise to much controversy. This is far from being an exhaustive list of topics for attention in the future.

The following fifteen chapters, while not aiming to be a comprehensive coverage of the subject of child abuse, deal with many of the most important topics from medical, legal and social work perspectives.

I am grateful to Angela Hodes, barrister of Lamb Building, Temple, for assisting with the editing of this book.

REFERENCES

1. A. Levy (ed.), *Focus on Child Abuse* (London, Hawksmere, 1989).
2. Lord Clyde, *The Report of the Inquiry into the Removal of Children from Orkney in February 1991* (London, HMSO, 1992).
3. A. Levy QC and B. Kahan, *The Pindown Experience and the Protection of Children: The Report of the Staffordshire Child Care Inquiry* (Staffordshire CC, 1991).

4. A. Kirkwood QC, *The Leicestershire Inquiry 1992* (Leicestershire Social Services, 1993); and *Inquiry into Police Investigation of Complaints of Child and Sexual Abuse in Leicestershire Children's Homes* (Police Complaints Authority, 1993).
5. Dame E. Butler-Sloss, *Report of the Inquiry into Child Abuse in Cleveland (1987)*, Cm 412 (London, HMSO, 1988).
6. *Rochdale BC* v. *A and others* [1991] 2 FLR 192.
7. Treaty Series No. 44 of 1992 (Cm 1976), adopted by the UN General Assembly on 20 November 1989. Ratified so far by 154 countries.

1

Child Abuse: the Approach of the Court

Dame Elizabeth Butler-Sloss
Lord Justice of Appeal

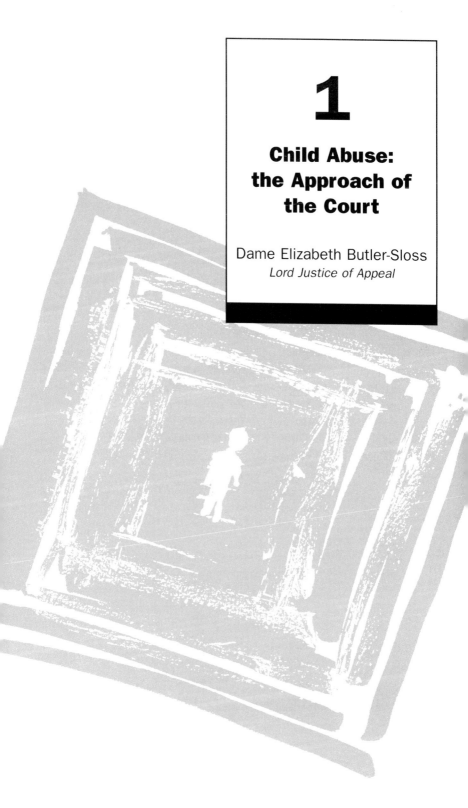

The impact of the Children Act 1989 and its attendant regulations on child civil law is still at an early stage. In looking at the approach of the courts to the problems of child abuse it is important to remember that the new structure has been in force for just over two years. The implications of the new legislation have not yet been fully explored; for example, the new threshold of judicial intervention in care applications and the appropriate use of the facility to make no order. Judges, the Bar and solicitors engaged in this work have already had considerable training in the ramifications of the Act and we would all benefit from further study. As with all new legislation, one problem is the extent to which, if at all, earlier legislation or case law is still applicable. Almost all the previous legislation other than with regard to adoption has been swept away but some of the earlier decisions remain relevant, to which I shall refer later.

Some things remain the same: children continue to be abused in various ways and often within the family circle. The impression I have is that abuse is more readily detected and responded to than in former days, but not that there is more abuse.

THE CRIMINAL COURTS

There remain, as before, two jurisdictions to respond to allegations of child abuse – the criminal courts and the civil courts – and not only their objectives but also their approach to the child victim remain markedly different. The objective of the criminal court is to prosecute the wrongdoer who is innocent until proved guilty. The child, the focus of the trial, may be and often is a witness but is not centre stage. The welfare of the child is not paramount and in many ways is subordinated to the rights of the accused. Much has been done to improve the lot of the child witness: the introduction of the initial video-recorded interview; the opportunity for the child to give evidence by a television link; and a child can give evidence without being sworn and his or her evidence can be accepted by a court without corroboration. These are, however, effectively procedural improvements to assist the witness and do not affect the heart of the problem – the place of the welfare of the child in the prosecution itself. The Pigot Report has been only partially implemented and a child is still likely to be required to give oral evidence and be cross-examined in the criminal trial. This requirement has had adverse consequences in a number of widely publicised cases, both for the child and for the prosecution case. I do not wish to underestimate the importance of the right of the accused, facing serious allegations, to test the evidence of the child who made them. That long-established right of the accused has, however, in my view to be balanced against the underrated importance of the welfare of the child in criminal trials. The dilemma has not yet been resolved and merits much greater consideration.

One aspect of welfare which appears not to have changed in some areas at least is the considerable difficulty for social workers and doctors in being allowed to work with children who may need assistance prior to the trial of the accused since such work may be seen to contaminate the evidence the child may have to give. If criminal trials were always able to be heard quickly this denial of assistance to the child might not be serious, but on occasions criminal trials are considerably delayed, to the child's detriment. The courts have held that the criminal trial should not be allowed to hold up the decision as to the child's future in the civil court hearing care proceedings. That principle is excellent as far as it goes but it may not be practical in those cases where the allegations against members of the family are so serious, such as murder which is totally denied, that it may be impossible to have a proper hearing of the care proceedings where the accused has not yet been before the jury.

Another issue which arises for a child whose parent or carer is accused of serious abuse, is whether to prosecute at all, and if so, the effect upon the child of the sentence to be imposed. Although crown court judges do, no doubt, have the welfare of the child in mind, it is not their duty to do so. There may be cases where the best interests of the child are incompatible with the duty to sentence. There are so far, to my knowledge, no guidelines in sentencing that require consideration of the child victim in the mode of sentence.

These are unresolved issues for the courts which appear to me to be unaffected by the new legislation.

HEARING THE CHILD

The Children Act has given statutory force to a growing realisation in the courts, from Lord Denning in the 1960s to Lord Scarman in the Gillick case in 1985, of the right of older children to be heard on matters affecting them. Section 1(3) states: 'A court shall have regard in particular to (a) the ascertainable wishes and feelings of the child concerned (considered in the light of his age and understanding)'. This subsection applies to part IV of the Act and consequently to cases involving, *inter alia*, child abuse in the public sector. It also applies to private law in part II, where there has been an increase in the number of allegations of abuse between parents of children who are the subject of their disputes.

Under the Act a child has the right to make applications, for instance, to discharge the care order or emergency protection order, to apply for contact or to refuse contact with a named person. On an application for a child assessment order or an emergency protection order, a child 'of sufficient understanding to make an informed decision' may refuse to submit to a medical or psychiatric examination or other assessment. By contrast, the Family Law Reform Act 1969 provides that a child who has reached the age of 16 may consent to medical treatment without the necessity of parental consent. That section does not refer to the right to refuse consent. There is, as I have already set out above, the general duty of the court to consider the wishes of the child.

It is still comparatively recently that the courts have had to consider the maturity of a child and its relevance to his or her ability to make decisions or express views. How is a court to make that assessment, upon what basis and with how much information? Age and maturity do not go hand in hand, and younger children may have a clearer and more credible viewpoint than many teenagers. Depending on the seriousness of the allegations and the circumstances of the child, the court may have to invoke expert evidence as to the maturity and understanding of the child, recognising that the refusal of a child, for instance, to be examined, is not necessarily an indication of immaturity. To my knowledge, there have been no reported cases in the public law sector on the ascertainment of a child's maturity and understanding but the issue has arisen in several cases tried on common law principles where the Court of Appeal has overridden the wishes of teenage children. These decisions are not entirely easy to reconcile with the perceived philosophy of the Children Act. The facts related to very serious medical conditions; for example, anorexia and leukaemia with an urgent need for a blood transfusion. To some extent the decisions turned upon the insufficient understanding of the implications by the child, but also upon a distinction between the effect of refusal to undergo treatment and the consent to such treatment. In each of the cases the overriding concern of the court was to protect the life of the child which was threatened by a failure to treat, rather than to enhance his wellbeing. In the context of examination and assessment, however, under the Children Act, Parliament has given the child the opportunity to say no. If found to be of sufficient understanding to make an informed decision, the loss of the opportunity to make an assessment, for instance, of sexual abuse may be exactly what was intended by the child, and the child protection team and the court may not have the evidence to find abuse proved. That is a situation with which all those involved in child protection have to learn to live.

REPRESENTATION OF THE CHILD

In most care applications the court will appoint a guardian ad litem for the child. The Court of Appeal has held that it is most undesirable for a child to be represented by a guardian ad litem and also for a court welfare officer to report since there is a considerable degree of overlap between the two functions. If a child has sufficient understanding to instruct a solicitor and wishes to do so, and the court considers that it would be in the child's best interests for him or her to be so represented, the court may appoint a solicitor to act for the child. The right of a child to have his or her own lawyer in care proceedings has not yet been tested in the appellate courts but in an analogous situation a child of 11, represented by the Official Solicitor in wardship proceedings, was refused his own solicitor (*Re S (A Minor) (Independent Representation)* [1993] 2 WLR 810). Sir Thomas Bingham, Master of the Rolls, said at p. 813:

> The Act of 1989 enables and requires a judicious balance to be struck between two considerations. First is the principle, to be honoured and respected, that children are human beings in their own right with individual minds and wills, views and emotions, which should command serious attention. A child's wishes are not to be discounted or dismissed simply because he is a child. He should be free to express them and decision-makers should listen. Second is the fact that a child is, after all, a child. The reason why the law is particularly solicitous in protecting the interests of children is because they are liable to be vulnerable and impressionable, lacking the maturity to weigh the longer term against the shorter, lacking the insight to know how they will react and the imagination to know how others will react in certain situations, lacking the experience to measure the probable against the possible. Everything of course depends on the individual child in his actual situation ... The judge has to do his best, on the evidence before him, to assess the understanding of the individual child in the context of the proceedings in which he seeks to participate.

In the light of the decision of the Court of Appeal in *Re S*, there may well be cases where the court will in future have to decide with some care whether it would be in the child's best interests to have his or her own solicitor, even if the child is of sufficient understanding to instruct the solicitor. It would seem, however, to me that an older child wishing to bring proceedings, such as to have contact with a member of the family rather than take part in proceedings brought by others, is likely to require his or her own representation.

In private family applications, on the other hand, the child can only make application with leave of the court and the President of the Family Division has directed that such applications are to be heard by a High Court judge. Consequently the child has no right to intervene in allegations of abuse forming part of the family dispute unless it enters the public arena with the intervention of the local authority. This distinction seems to me entirely appropriate since the consequences to the child of a decision in part IV proceedings may be much more dramatic and far reaching than a decision within the family.

THE CHILD'S EVIDENCE

Although the child is an essential party to care proceedings and will either be represented by a guardian ad litem or his or her own lawyers, it is not yet the practice for children to give evidence; indeed the trend is the other way. However, it seems clear that some children, notably in recent publicised decisions in the United States, want to play their own part in the decision-making process. We are moving slowly towards greater participation by children in the proceedings and it may not be long before the courts may have to give ground on protecting children from a situation from which they do not wish to be protected. There is a dilemma here also. For many children the giving of oral evidence in the care court would be nearly as traumatic as the criminal trial. In each case it would include cross-examination and challenge to the evidence given by the child. Other children wish to play a more effective role than being interviewed at an earlier stage. A few already give evidence. They may wish to support the accusations; some at least would wish to support the denial of such accusations and support their family for a number of reasons, not necessarily to arrive at the truth. We are still at an early stage in recognising the place of the child in the court procedure.

In the past, in wardship cases, the judge on occasions saw the child privately in his or her room. This was sometimes a most revealing and indeed decisive interview but it has grave disadvantages. There was no opportunity for the advocates to monitor the child's conversation with the judge and they had to rely upon the judge giving a summary of the interview in court. Also the procedure was haphazard in that some judges did not like to see children and others did. It would be very difficult to devise a suitable procedure without either causing the child the very stress it was intended to avoid or denying to the parties the opportunity to correct the impression made by the child on the judge. Also it would be an unsuitable procedure for a court of two or three magistrates or indeed the Court of Appeal. Although I personally enjoyed meeting children in my room, other than on non-controversial occasions such as adoption, in my view the future attendance of a child in the civil court ought to be at least in the presence of the advocates and with some degree of procedural formality.

In the majority of cases, which so far come before the courts, the evidence of the children and their wishes are presented by others both in written and oral form. The Hearsay Order has enormously simplified the process of bringing evidence relating to children before the courts. However, the Court of Appeal has warned that the order is not to be used in proceedings designed to deal with the adults where the interests of the children are not immediate, such as breaches of injunctions not referring to the children.

In care proceedings the evidence of the child will be relevant to the findings of the existence of abuse. There has been shown to be a danger that the accusations of abuse by children or evidence consistent with abuse are believed by the child protection team, whereas a child's denials of abuse have from time to time been treated as pressure on the child rather than the possibility that the abuse did not occur. This approach of the professionals has been criticised not only in the Cleveland and Orkney Reports but also in a long line of judicial decisions in the Court of Appeal and the Family Division of the High Court. The interview with the child is of the utmost importance and is much more useful if it has been efficiently video-recorded with a transcript so that the court may both read what the child said and see the sometimes most revealing way in which it was said or demonstrated. The child's account has to be carefully assessed by the court in the context of all the other relevant evidence.

Where there are serious allegations of abuse of whatever form, the wishes of the child are likely to play a less important part in the decision of the court than in the private law dispute between parents. The emphasis in abuse cases is upon protection. Unless the child made allegations that were not substantiated, in which case it may be necessary to look at the interaction of the family, or there are other grounds sufficient for the s. 31 threshold to be reached, if abuse is not proved, the child goes home. If abuse is proved and it is within the family circle, the wish of the child to go home is one factor in the equation of exercising the discretion of the court, but the need to protect the child outside the family may prove more powerful. In all cases the child has to be listened to, but in care cases in particular, his or her wishes will often not be decisive.

THE COURTS

It has been said, and I hope it is true, that the present procedure of the family courts is designed to incorporate the best of the wardship jurisdiction. The court is expected to be interventionist and, most important of all, to have control over the applications and the way in which they will be presented: over the timetables (subject to unavoidable delays); over the documents and witnesses to be called; and in being able to call for further information. All lawyers engaged in a child case ought to have in their minds the concept of the welfare of the child as the paramount consideration, and should moderate their adversarial inclinations accordingly. But in these very serious and fraught applications alleging child abuse, there remains a duty upon the lawyers for the adult accused of such behaviour to test and often challenge the evidence adduced. It will be for the court to intervene to curb an over-enthusiastic or unsuitable stance taken by an advocate in a child case. The court may invite a local authority to intervene in a family case where, for instance, serious abuse is an issue, although it has only limited influence over the decision of the local authority whether actually to take part.

A major consequence of the new Act is the transfer of control in the making of a care order from the court to the local authority in all cases unless or until a further application is made. A court can no longer review the working of a care order. This policy decision has tidied up previous inconsistent procedures and has dealt a seemingly mortal blow to the use of wardship in public law cases. It remains to be seen how far and in what circumstances the High Court will exercise its inherent jurisdiction.

THE EFFECT OF PRE-CHILDREN ACT DECISIONS

The threshold criteria for making a care or supervision order have entirely changed and consequently the decisions based on the wording of previous legislation are no longer relevant for that purpose. However, the Court of Appeal has stated (in *Newham LBC* v. *AG* [1993] 1FLR 281) that the approach to care applications under s. 31 is similar to and does not lay down a stricter test than that laid down in s. 7(2) of the Family Law Reform Act 1969. In his judgment Sir Stephen Brown, President, added (at p. 288) that the courts ought not to be invited to perform a strict legalistic analysis of the statutory meaning of s. 31. Earlier decisions on the standard of proof of the evidence adduced, that is to say on the balance of probabilities, but commensurate with the seriousness of the allegations made, still bind the family courts. The approach of the court to a care application based upon allegations of abuse still requires the evaluation of the evidence adduced and findings whether the child has been abused, and if so, whether it is possible to identify the abuser on the civil standard of proof. In any event, if the court has found that the child was abused, it must assess the future risk to the child and whether he or she is likely to suffer significant harm. In applying considerations as to the approach of the court to the assessment of future risk, earlier decisions of the Court of Appeal are still relevant. Equally, decisions based upon evidence called in abuse cases and the caution with which such evidence that has not been subjected to cross-examination requires to be weighed, remain highly pertinent.

In the light of the complete control by a local authority of future plans for a child in care, the extent to which a court ought to make orders which may be incompatible with long-term plans raises a delicate and potentially troublesome issue. The Court of Appeal has held (in *Re B (Minors) (Care: Contact: Local Authority's Plans)* [1993] 1FLR 543) that, although the principle in *A* v. *Liverpool City Council* that the court has no reviewing power over the exercise of the local authority's discretionary decisions was still applicable, it did not apply to the intervention of the court in response to an application under the Children Act. The exercise of judicial discretion provided by part I of the Act was not fettered. In the context of a contact application, the court could ask the local authority to justify its plans insofar as they might exclude contact between the child and the family, and the court could make an order for contact which would be incompatible with those long-term plans. It would be most unusual for that situation to arise, but earlier decisions to the contrary are not now applicable.

THE FUTURE

The Children Act has created an entirely new structure which requires time to operate effectively. It would be wrong, in my view, to seek at this stage to suggest fundamental changes. When the proposed divorce legislation comes up for consideration there would be the opportunity to put right some areas of concern. For instance, in domestic violence situations where there are children they are likely to suffer, whether or not it can be said to be sufficiently serious to use the terminology of abuse. It would be a useful card in the judicial pack to have the option to exclude one parent for a limited period, in the interests of the children, rather than the other parent leaving with the children, thus causing upheaval and upset. I should also like to see the alleged abuser leave home for a limited period and, if necessary, assisted financially rather than the child taken away from home and placed in care for what may be a temporary period.

Should we continue to have an adversarial system in family cases? Particularly in abuse cases, with the need to establish the correct facts to meet the threshold criteria without which the best interests of the child may not arise, a wholly inquisitorial system would place the burden entirely upon the court, or else an independent prosecutor would have to present the case. The latter would be expensive and not necessarily effective. There are, in my view, grave disadvantages in expecting the court to ask all the questions, with the danger of descending into the arena. There are also great advantages for the court in sitting back and watching a witness being cross-examined, and having time to assess personality, temperament and credibility. As I said above, I would not wish to lose the advantages of the adversarial system but I should like to see it tailored to the special needs of the family courts. For example, if there is evidence available which is relevant to the issue before the court, it should be made available to the court even if adverse to the party who has obtained it. The court ought to have the power to call for such evidence as, under wardship, it was able to do. There are differing views in the High Court as to whether this power already exists. If it does not, it should be made available and the court should be provided with adequate tools to be able to act flexibly in the best interests of the child.

Should a judge sit alone or with assessors to try child cases? The magistrates sit as three and I can see the obvious advantages of collegiate decisions. The judges, however, will now be trying the more serious cases transferred to them under the allocation procedure. All the cases are likely to be difficult, many with a multiplicity of parties and a stack of written documents. They already take at least several days, often several weeks and sometimes months. For the judges, now specifically designated to try this difficult work, it would be easier to work alone and almost certainly a lot quicker. I can see no convincing reason to change the existing procedure of the judge sitting alone.

I would like to repeat my strongly held view that more needs to be done for the child, the victim of abuse, in the criminal courts which are not designed to consider his or her interests. I should like to see the Pigot Report implemented in full. We have seen in Cleveland and in Orkney, among other inquiries, that one category of abuse could be caused by those intending to help children. It would be a sad reflection upon our administration of justice if one way in which we seek to protect children from abusers and enforce the law by prosecuting the offenders turns out to be a further administrative abuse of the child.

2

Legislating for Child Abuse: the Children Act and Significant Harm

Professor M. D. A. Freeman

The Children Act 1989 does not, as such, define child abuse. Nor does *Working Together*,[1] although this, at least, attempts a categorisation of the phenomena involved. But the categories listed there (neglect, physical injury, sexual abuse and emotional abuse) do not fit precisely into the mould of the Children Act, where the trigger for intervention is 'significant harm'.[2]

It is upon this concept that the civil law programme for tackling child abuse hinges.[3] Embedded within the concept is part of the philosophy of the Act: as explained by the Lord Chancellor, 'the integrity and independence' of the family are the 'basic building blocks of a free and democratic society'. The result of this thinking is that 'unless there is evidence that a child is being or is likely to be positively harmed because of a failure in the family, the state, whether in the guise of a local authority or court, should not interfere'.[4] Even if a local authority (or the NSPCC)[5] makes an application for care and proves the minimum threshold condition, the court is only supposed to make a care order if making the order will be better for the child than making no order at all.[6] The presumption of no order ties in with the pro-family stance in the Act, where the emphasis is on partnership[7] and parental responsibility.[8]

A care order is only one way – indeed the most drastic – of protecting an abused child by using the Children Act. Children at risk may be given temporary relief by means of emergency protection orders,[9] and a child assessment order[10] may be sought where there is concern, if no hard evidence. Indeed, in an Act as integrated as the Children Act is, a whole panoply of measures can be brought to bear to protect children. In private law proceedings a court may direct an authority to undertake an investigation of the child's circumstances with a view to bringing an application for a care or supervision order.[11] Whether this power is strong enough may be doubted:[12] whether it is used sufficiently may be questioned. But it is there and it is potentially of great value where concern about a child's welfare arises in any family proceedings[13] – a case of domestic violence,[14] for example. Indirectly, a private law order such as a residence order[15] can be used to protect a child against abuse, for example by placing an abused child or one at risk of abuse with a grandparent or other relative. An essay on child abuse and the Children Act could thus become an essay on the Children Act. This temptation will be resisted. This chapter concentrates in particular on the care order, with a little attention also given to emergency protection. The emphasis will be on the way in which the courts are interpreting significant harm.

This is the trigger for care (and supervision) and also the concept upon which other coercive intervention (emergency protection and child assessment) hinges. There is now only one route into care, requiring proof of the minimum threshold conditions set out in s. 31(2). The fall-back of wardship, positively encouraged by the courts[16] for so long, where local authorities felt that the statutory framework did not offer children sufficient protection, is now drastically curtailed.[17] It is possible that, as a result, some cases may fall through the safety net: indeed, that the 1989 legislation may fail to protect some children whom a combination of the 1969 Act and wardship would have protected.[18] The 1989 Act, however, rests on legality and emphasises rights rather than deploying broad welfarist notions.

THRESHOLD FOR INTERVENTION

The new minimum conditions create a threshold for intervention which must be surmounted before coercive intervention into child-rearing is countenanced. The conditions (or 'criteria' as the *Guidance* calls them)[19] are found in s. 31(2). This subsection contains the most complex interpretational problems in the whole Act.[20] The conditions are as follows:

A court may only make a care order or supervision order if it is satisfied –
(a) that the child concerned is suffering, or is likely to suffer, significant harm; and (b) that the harm, or likelihood of harm, is attributable to –

(i) the care given to the child, or likely to be given to him if the order were not made, not being what it would be reasonable to expect a parent to give to him, or

(ii) the child's being beyond parental control.

SIGNIFICANT HARM

The linchpin of care is thus 'significant harm'. What does this mean? In particular, what is 'significant' for these purposes? The DHSS *Review of Child Care Law*[21] stated:

> Having set an acceptable standard of upbringing for the child, it should be necessary to show some substantial deficit in that standard. Minor shortcomings in the health and care provided or minor defects in physical, psychological or social development should not give rise to any compulsory intervention unless they are having, or likely to have, serious and lasting effects upon the child.

The focus is thus on 'substantial deficit'. The *Guidance* to the Act[22] quotes the dictionary definition of 'considerable, noteworthy or important'. The standard thus seems lower than 'severe', perhaps even lesser than 'serious'. Harm may be significant in a number of ways: in amount, in effect, in importance. The *Guidance* is not over-helpful. We are told[23] that significance can exist 'in the seriousness of the harm or in the implications of it'. It passes the buck to the courts: it will, it says, 'be a finding of fact for the court'.[24]

One pre-Children Act case (*Re B*)[25] did, I think, offer considerable assistance, although the judge was not, of course, interpreting 'significant harm'. The case concerned a 4-year-old boy who had been sexually abused by his father. Ward J referred to a 'spectrum of abuse' and an 'index of harm' in a judgment of real sensitivity which offers insight into what is meant by 'significant' harm. The fact that it was a loving, stable home, and that there was an excellent relationship between the mother and the boy, both of whom were devastated by the rupture caused by the abuse, led the judge to conclude that the boy could be safely reintegrated into the family.

A lesson of this is that 'significant' has to be situated within relationships. It is necessary to look at *this* child within the context of *this* home: abuse in one context is not necessarily abuse in another. And context must also include culture. There is a diversity of cultural arrangements for child-rearing. Nevertheless, it is clearly imperative that the state establishes 'boundaries of minimal adequacy',[26] however problematic this may be.[27] Parliament has thus declared female circumcision practices, common among certain African peoples, to be unacceptable.[28] But we would not expect it to place the same sanction on male circumcision, although there is a lobby[29] which rather naively analogises this to the outlawed female circumcision (or genital mutilation) practices.

The Children Act uses 'significant harm' as the trigger for intervention. But it should not be overlooked that 'insignificant' harm may also be significant in that it may alert to the risk of 'significant harm' occurring in the future. Moderate corporal chastisement may not cause significant harm. It can lead, however, almost inexorably, to the infliction of more severe punishment. The line between legitimate corporal punishment and child abuse is, at best, fuzzy.[30] Too many of the notorious child death cases are exercises of discipline which have gone badly wrong. It is doubtful whether we will ever eliminate child abuse until we also recognise, as the Nordic countries and Austria already do,[31] that hitting a child is wrong, and should be unlawful.

MEANING OF HARM

'Harm' itself is broadly defined in the Act. It means 'ill-treatment' or the 'impairment of health and development' (s. 31(9)). In the Lords, the Lord Chancellor explained 'ill-treatment' thus: it 'is not a precise term and would include, for example, instances of verbal abuse or unfairness falling a long way short of significant harm'.[32] The examples he gives are instructive – particularly in that they emphasise 'emotional' rather than 'physical' trauma – but his statement cannot be taken at face value: clearly, if the acts fall short of significant harm, they cannot form the basis of a care application.

The Act defines 'ill-treatment' as including sexual abuse and forms of ill-treatment that are not physical (s. 31(9)). It includes physical abuse by implication. This was, of course, the earliest form of child abuse to be socially recognised, emerging in the early 1960s as Henry Kempe's 'battered baby syndrome'[33] and later being broadened to embrace all 'non-accidental injuries' to children.[34] The *Guidance* advises[35] that ill-treatment is sufficient proof of harm in itself, so that it is 'not necessary to show that impairment of health or development has followed, or is likely to follow (though that might be relevant to later stages of the test)'.

Although not specifically mentioned, 'emotional abuse' (listed in the *Working Together* document)[36] is clearly an example of non-physical ill-treatment. Emotional abuse was recognised as embraced by the concept of 'being ill-treated' for the purposes of the 1969 legislation.[37] Since then our awareness and understanding of emotional abuse have been heightened considerably.[38] Unlike other forms of abuse, the focus is on the child's abnormal behaviour, rather than on abnormal parenting. There is thus a problem where the 'abuse' has resulted in no discernible disturbance in the child.

Sexual abuse is specifically included within 'ill-treatment', but not as such defined in the Act. In C v. C,[39] a pre-Children Act case, the father was said to have indulged in 'vulgar and inappropriate horseplay' with his daughter. Is this sexual abuse or not? Where is the line to be drawn, and by whom? Our attitudes to sexual abuse clearly differ, as the battlelines drawn over Cleveland indicate.[40] There is, not surprisingly, no universally accepted definition of what constitutes sexual abuse.[41] Proof of harm may be difficult to establish: indeed, the courts seem to believe that the standard of proof in child sexual abuse cases should be higher than in other abuse cases.[42]

The Children Act does not define what is meant by 'ill-treatment'. It includes sexual abuse and non-physical ill-treatment. But what else? The 1969 Act had a separate category of 'neglect', and this is not listed in s. 31. Under the old law, failure to obtain medical treatment would have been considered 'neglect'.[43] We must assume now that it is either 'ill-treatment' or 'the impairment of health or development', probably in most cases the latter.

When is corporal punishment ill-treatment? English law has long separated sanctioned punishment from abuse with the vague test of 'moderate and reasonable'.[44] It seems, accordingly, that hitting a child is not ill-treatment so long as it does not exceed, in intensity or duration, what a reasonable parent might do. Also, it must be inflicted for disciplinary reasons and not to indulge in gratification.[45] We cannot indicate in advance what constitutes moderate and reasonable punishment and the standards are continually changing. Abuse in this context is thus a label applied retrospectively. To some this may offend against legality: one response is that those who skate on thin ice cannot expect a sign to alert them to the exact point where the ice will cave in.

PAST, PRESENT AND FUTURE

The minimum conditions state that the child 'is suffering, or is likely to suffer significant harm'. The Act thus concentrates on present abuse and risk of future abuse. The latter is important: the previous legislation had not been forward-looking in this way, thus requiring local authorities to seek protection through wardship.[46] The need for wardship is to some extent obviated by the language of s. 31(2), which allows a care order to be sought where the prognosis is that the child is likely to suffer significant harm.

The courts have held that they are not limited only to looking at the present and the immediate future. In a case[47] that centred on the ability of a lesbian couple to bring up a baby girl, the court concluded that if a parent, or carer, was likely to be unable to meet the emotional needs of a child in the future, even if years hence, the conditions in s. 31(2) would 'probably be met'.[48] This was expressed by the judge as a 'provisional view' and takes a rather pessimistic view about the ability of a carer to learn; however, as another court has held, parents can learn, but children should not have to wait.[49]

The phrase 'likely to suffer' has caused another court to indulge in mental gymnastics. In *Newham LBC v. AG*,[50] the President of the Family Division said that it was wrong to equate 'likely to suffer' with 'on a balance of probabilities'.[51] He said that when looking to the future, all the court could do was evaluate the chances. But, since such an evaluation must inevitably assess probabilities, the difference is far from clear. The President in this case also made a pronouncement about interpretation of the Act generally which, though protective of children, strikes me as dangerous, if not heretical. He hoped that 'in approaching cases under the Act, courts would not be invited to perform in every case a strict legalistic analysis of the statutory meaning of section 31. The words of the statute', he said, 'must be considered, but they were not intended to be unduly restrictive when evidence clearly indicated that a certain course should be taken in order to protect the child.'[52]

The phrase 'is suffering' has interpretational difficulties as well. In interpreting the 1969 Act, the House of Lords had to confront these in the 'heroin addict' mother case (*Re D*).[53] In that case Lord Goff of Chievely had said: 'The words "is being" are in the continuous present. So there has to be a continuum in existence at the relevant time, which is when the magistrates consider whether to make a place of safety order.'[54] Lord Brandon of Oakbrook, by contrast, had said: 'The court, in considering whether a continuing situation ... exists, must do so as at the point of time immediately before the process of protecting the child concerned is first put into motion.'[55] These tests are not the same, although the difference did not trouble Lord Mackay of Clashfern or Lord Griffiths who agreed with both. Given that months or longer may elapse between the initial protective steps and the court being asked to make an order, the difference is not merely semantic. On Lord Goff's test, the child must be suffering at the time the court is asked to make its order: on Lord Brandon's, at the time immediately before the first action was taken. If Parliament had wanted to adopt Lord Brandon's test it could have added 'has suffered' to 'is suffering'. It is, of course, anyway open to a court to decide on the evidence of past suffering that a child is 'likely to suffer' in the future, even if that child is not suffering significant harm now.

The courts have had three opportunities to consider the meaning of 'is suffering' since the Children Act came into operation. In *Northamptonshire CC* v. *S*,[56] Ewbank J followed Lord Brandon. He said: 'The words "is suffering" in section 31(2) (a) ... relate to the period immediately before the process of protecting the child concerned is first put into motion ...'[57] In *Re B*,[58] *Re D* was not cited, and Douglas Brown J relied on Butler-Sloss J (as she then was) in *M* v. *Westminster CC*.[59] Having first decided, rather extraordinarily, that he did not have to be satisfied that the 'circumstances' in s. 31(2) 'exist in fact',[60] he held that the court was not confined to facts only existing at the date of the hearing, by which point the child had been removed from any conceivable possibility of harm. The use of the present continuous indicated, he said, following Butler-Sloss J, a situation over a period of time sufficiently proximate to the date of the inquiry to indicate that it was a present and continuing set of circumstances, and not mere history of possible future events. The Butler-Sloss phrase 'mere history of possible future events' has been repeated so often that I assume someone must know what it means. I do not. It would appear that Douglas Brown J is allying himself with the Brandon view.[61]

The third case, and the only one to reach the Court of Appeal, is *Re M*.[62] The court held that a court could not make a care order on the grounds that the child is suffering significant harm if the child had ceased to suffer such harm before the hearing. Balcombe LJ, giving the judgment of the court, specifically adopted Lord Goff's reasoning and overruled the *Northamptonshire* case. *Re B* does not appear to have been cited. *Re M* arose out of the murder by the father of the mother and a conflict which then erupted between the father and the guardian ad litem on the one hand (the latter purporting to represent the child's interests) and the deceased mother's cousin who was seeking a residence order. The father and the guardian ad litem wanted a care order with a view to adoption. The Court of Appeal rejected the 'social engineering' implied in the father's case – and, in my view, was quite right to do so. It has, therefore, to be taken to be the law that 'is suffering' means what it says, and a care order cannot be made after harm to the child has ceased, unless past harm is prognostic of future risk of harm.

THE 'SIMILAR' CHILD

One of the most difficult questions centres on the notion of a 'similar' child. Section 31(10) states: 'Where the question of whether harm suffered by a child is significant turns on the child's health or development, his health or development shall be compared with that which could be reasonably expected of a similar child.' The comparator is a 'similar child', not a child of similar parents. The standard of care below which parents must not fall is that which can be reasonably expected to be given to similar children.

What is a 'similar child'? According to the Lord Chancellor, it is a child with the same physical attributes as the child concerned, and not a child of the same background. On this test, the development of a 4-year-old has to be compared with that of other 4-year-olds, and not with other 4-year-olds from similar backgrounds.[63] If this interpretation is right, a child from a deprived background is expected to achieve intellectual growth and emotional maturity comparable to children who come from well-ordered, materially comfortable and stimulating environments. The *Guidance*, on the other hand, says that we 'may' need to 'take account of environmental, social and cultural characteristics of the child'.[64] Neither view has any legal authority, but the latter is, I would submit, preferable.

There are thus problems with the term 'similar child'. But what the phrase does achieve is the comparison of *this* child with children like him or her, that is with children with the same attributes. So, to take an example, the development of a deaf 4-year-old boy is to be compared with what is to be expected of other 4-year-olds who are deaf, and not with other 4-year-olds. But the value of this may be more apparent than real. So much depends on when the boy was diagnosed as deaf. There are differences of opinion on the right treatment and education. Much turns also on whether the parents are deaf. If we take account only of the characteristics of the child, as the subsection requires, a deaf child of deaf parents is like a deaf child of hearing parents, but, of course, he is not. His rearing will have taken place in a different environment: his parents, with experience of deafness, may well have attitudes to deafness and to the education of the deaf very different from parents who have not themselves suffered the disability. However laudatory the goal in emphasising the special needs of handicapped children, reliance on the concept of 'similar child' overlooks the essential individuality of families and their problems. By concentrating on the child, it also ignores the impact of interaction between the child and his or her parents.[65]

The courts hitherto have only interpreted the concept of 'similar child' in the unusual[66] circumstance of a school refusal case. In *Re O*,[67] 'similar child' was said to mean 'a child of equivalent intellectual and social development, who has gone to school, and not merely an average child who may or may not be at school'.

THE QUALITY OF CARE

The second limb of the minimum threshold condition requires the court to be satisfied that the harm or its likelihood is 'attributable to the care given to the child, or likely to be given to him if the order were not made, not being what it would be reasonable to expect a parent to give to him or the child's being beyond parental control'.[68]

The quality of care must fall below what it is reasonable to expect of a parent. 'Care' is not defined but must include catering for a child's total needs (physical, emotional, social, intellectual, behavioural) and not just having physical charge.[69] In *Re B*,[70] Douglas Brown J held that it included the emotional care that reasonable parents would give to their child. In the case of an abused child, that included listening to the child and monitoring his or her words and actions so that a professional assessment could be carried out.

The quality of care given to the child is not what it would be reasonable for *this* parent to give, but what it would be reasonable to expect *a* parent to give. The standard is objective: it concentrates on the 'needs of the child ... rather than on some hypothetical child and the hypothesis is transferred to the parent'.[71] The emphasis is on *this* child, given this child's needs. If the child has asthma or brittle bones,[72] he or she may need more care, or a different type of care, from a 'normal' child. If *a* parent could provide this, then *this* parent is failing if he or she cannot do so, particularly if such care cannot be accomplished even with support from appropriate community-wide services.[73]

The extent to which cultural pluralism should be taken into account is a matter of some contention. It is Bainham's view that the different situations of ethnic minority groups only become relevant when, the threshold condition having been satisfied, s. 1(3) comes into play with its checklist, which includes reference to the background of the child.[74] But, in legislation committed to cultural pluralism,[75] it ought to be asked whether the hypothetically reasonable parent has to be located within the dominant white English Christian culture. It might not be reasonable to expect *a* parent to have a male baby circumcised, but it would be unreasonable to expect a Jewish parent to do anything else. What is 'significant harm' depends upon cultural context. There is a line-drawing exercise involved. The courts have had to confront this very problem when dealing with the chastisement practices of ethnic minority groups. Thus, in *Re H*,[76] the practices of a mother, who was by origin Vietnamese, were judged against the 'reasonable objective standards of the culture in which the children hitherto have been brought up', although the judge was careful to add 'so long as these do not conflict with our minimal acceptable standards of child care in England'.

The harm must be 'attributable' to the quality of care given falling below what it would be reasonable to expect a parent to give. I have argued elsewhere[77] that 'attributable to' is not the same as 'caused by' – indeed, that it is wider. My view is supported by Douglas Brown J in *Re B*[78] who held that where an aunt impaired an assessment of whether a 4-year-old had been sexually abused by her father, there were reasonable grounds for believing that significant harm would be suffered and this was attributable to the care likely to be given to the girl by her aunt. It is difficult to see how the aunt's stubbornness could possibly have caused the girl significant harm.

Is the Order Better for the Child?

It is easy to see the threshold condition as the ground for care, but wrong to do so. A court which is satisfied that the condition is met needs also to be satisfied that the care order will be 'better' for the child than making no order (s. 1(5)). Even if the child is to continue to live at home or with extended family, it might be better for the child for the local authority to be in the 'driving seat', and a care order would give it this status. If the intention is to remove the child, there will need to be a clear plan and this, as the *Guidance* puts it, needs to be more than 'embryonic'.[79] There is too much foster care breakdown and too much abuse in care for anyone to believe that a care order is any kind of panacea.

But are the courts understanding this? Or are they making care orders when the threshold condition is proved, without deliberating about whether the order is right for the child? Are we asking the courts to undertake an evaluative process to which they are not accustomed and which they are understandably finding difficult? After all, courts see themselves as institutions that make orders. Is that not what they are for, after all?

One can look at reported judicial practice in two ways. There are cases that consider the implications of s. 1(5): *Humberside CC v. B*[80] is one example; *Essex CC v. B*[81] another, which decided that an education supervision order was better for a 14-year-old than no order because otherwise the situation would drift. But of greater interest are the cases where there does not appear to be any thought given to the implications of the presumption of non-intervention. There are cases where judges appear to assume that once the threshold conditions are proved, *cadit quaestio*. For example, in *Northamptonshire CC v. S*,[82] Ewbank J says that 'the justices have a choice once the threshold conditions are met of making a care order, of making a supervision order, or of making any other order under the Children Act 1989', but not, note, no order. In *Kent CC v. C*,[83] the same judge remarks: 'The mother and the guardian ad litem agreed that the conditions were met and accordingly there was *no contest* on the question of whether a care order should be made'[84] (the judge's emphasis). But the Act says 'when *a court* is considering whether or not to make [an] order ... *it* shall not make the order ... unless *it* considers that doing so would be better for the child ...' (my emphasis).

If these cases are but the tip of the iceberg, and the impression is being acquired that in Family Proceedings Courts in particular this is not untypical of daily practice (thus we know that less than 30 per cent of care applications result in orders of no order), how is s. 1(5) to be placed back upon the pinnacle where the legislation wanted it? Or do our judges and justices know better? Does ignoring the presumption of non-intervention better protect children?

THE PARAMOUNTCY PRINCIPLE

That in all matters relating to the upbringing of a child, that child's welfare is the paramount consideration, should 'determine the course to be followed',[85] governs the making of care orders as it does other orders (see s. 1(1)). The issue has arisen most intriguingly in the case of *Birmingham CC* v. *H* (No. 2).[86] Both the mother and the child were minors: the local authority wanted to stop contact between the mother and her son. This may well have been in his best interests, but was not necessarily in hers. Whose welfare is paramount, the mother's or the son's? The Court of Appeal held that neither should be given priority: the requirement in s. 1(1) has to be regarded as 'qualified, in the cases where the welfare of more than one child is involved, by the need to have regard to potential detriment for one in the light of potential benefit for the other'.[87] What this fails to address is the clear message in the Children Act, although it can be traced back to case law in 1973,[88] that contact is a child's right, not a parent's. Section 34 of the Children Act is couched in terms of the authority allowing *the child* reasonable contact with his or her parents (see s. 34(1)); an authority or the child may apply for an order authorising the authority to refuse to allow contact between *the child* and any person (see s. 34(4)). Evans LJ may not think that contact as a right of the child is a 'statement of principle'[89] (that much is obvious from his approval of Edmund Davies LJ in *B* v. *B*),[90] but the Children Act clearly does adopt it as one. Where there is a conflict between a parent-child and a child, there is little doubt in my mind that the correct interpretation of the Children Act will give priority to the interests of the child. It is to be hoped that the House of Lords will reverse the Court of Appeal.

INHERENT JURISDICTION

The decision to restrict wardship was taken late. It was, and was regarded by local authorities as, a useful weapon in the fight against child abuse. With its 'golden thread' putting the child's welfare 'first, last and all the time', it became a way of protecting children who might fall through the statutory net.[91] But s. 100(2) of the Children Act lays down that the inherent jurisdiction[92] of the High Court cannot be exercised to require a child to be placed in care, supervised by a local authority or accommodated by or on behalf of a local authority. If the local authority wishes to apply to the court for an order under inherent jurisdiction, it must obtain leave (s. 100(3)) and satisfy the conditions set out in s. 100(4). The court must be satisfied that the result could not be achieved by the local authority applying for an order other than by exercise of the court's inherent jurisdiction, and there is 'reasonable cause' to believe that the child will suffer significant harm if the jurisdiction is not exercised. It seems that the local authority has to satisfy the same test as for a care order, even though it does not wish to acquire parental responsibility.[93]

The restriction on wardship/inherent jurisdiction fits the philosophy of the Act, but is an uneasy compromise. Many, and not just local authorities, will reject the undermining of what was thought to be valuable, and undoubtedly did protect some victims of abuse who might not otherwise have been helped.

It is not surprising that the Court of Appeal should recently have stated[94] that s. 100(2) should not be interpreted in such a way as to prevent or discourage local authorities from exercising the right of having recourse to inherent jurisdiction in cases where its general powers under part IV of the Children Act are found, for some exceptional reasons, to be insufficient to enable it to carry out its duty under the Act (s. 17) to safeguard and promote the welfare of a child in its area who is 'in need'. And in *South Glamorgan CC v. W and B*,[95] Douglas Brown J was in no doubt that the court could, in an 'appropriate' and 'rare' case 'when other remedies within the Children Act have been used and exhausted and found not to bring about the desired result',[96] use the inherent jurisdiction. Such jurisdiction was there invoked to overrule a 15-year-old girl who refused to submit to treatment and assessment, which she had every right to do under the Children Act.[97] The decision to restrict wardship, to circumscribe it and hedge it about, as the judge put it in the South Glamorgan case,[98] was taken precipitately and it is clear that some of the judges are bucking against that decision. But, as *South Glamorgan CC v. W and B* also illustrates, and the more notorious decisions of *Re R*[99] and *Re W*[100] aptly demonstrate, the judiciary is also uncomfortable with the implications of the Gillick[101] decision of 1985. But is not removing rights from adolescents[102] itself a covert form of child abuse?

EMERGENCY PROTECTION

Part V of the Children Act offers a framework for the investigation of abuse and the speedy protection of children who may be at risk. England does not have mandatory reporting of child abuse.[103] Under s. 47 of the Children Act, local authorities have a duty to make, or cause to be made, enquiries where they are informed that there is a child in their area who is subject to an emergency protection order or in police protection, or they have reasonable cause to suspect that there is a child in their area who is suffering, or likely to suffer, significant harm. Their enquiries are to enable them to decide whether they should take any action to safeguard or promote the child's welfare. The local authority clearly has a discretion but the enquiries must, in particular, be directed towards establishing whether they should make any application to the court or exercise any other of their powers (in particular those in part III of the Act).[104]

The child assessment order (CAO) is designed for the situation where there is fear for a child's health, development or safety, but no hard evidence. According to the *Guidance*,[105] a CAO will usually be most appropriate where the harm is 'long-term and cumulative rather than sudden and severe' (sexual abuse will often come into this category). The *Guidance* stresses[106] that a CAO is 'emphatically not for emergencies'. The effect of a CAO is that the child must be produced (see s. 43(6)(a)) and an assessment can be carried out. The court can allow up to seven days for the assessment. The *Guidance* recommends that the applicant (local authority or NSPCC) should make the necessary arrangements in advance of the application, 'so that it would usually be possible to complete within [the seven days] an initial multi-disciplinary assessment of the child's medical, intellectual, social and behavioural needs'. This, says the *Guidance*, 'should be sufficient to establish whether the child is suffering, or is likely to suffer, significant harm and, if so, what further action is required'.[107] Experience suggests, as was anticipated, that this is misplaced optimism. Few child assessment orders are being sought.

Emergency protection orders (EPOs) replaced the place of safety order. The purpose of an EPO is to enable a child in a genuine emergency to be removed from the place where he or she is or retained where he or she currently is (for example, a hospital), if and only if this is what is necessary to provide immediate short-term protection. The court (unlike with a CAO, where it may be a single justice) has to be satisfied that the child is likely to suffer significant harm or cannot be seen in circumstances where he or she might be suffering significant harm (s. 44(1)). Applications may be *ex parte*, and even oral. The order lasts for eight days, with one possible extension of seven days. As was said of place of safety orders,[108] the granting of the order should be 'a discretionary judicial act', although most justices will err on the side of safety, even if 'rubber-stamping' has ceased. The *Guidance* stresses that an application for an EPO is 'an extremely serious step' and should not be regarded as 'a routine response to allegations of child abuse or a routine first step to initiating care proceedings'.[109] Local authorities are expected to explore alternatives to seeking an EPO. The use of accommodation for the child

(s. 20) or the abuser (schedule 2, para. 5) is one possibility. Encouraging the non-abusing parent to seek an ouster order against the abuser is another.[110] Mooted and expected domestic violence legislation may well provide further ouster remedies which will be welcomed by those who believe that removing the abuser is a better expedient than taking the child away from home.

The police also have an important role in child protection.[111] The Children Act recognises this in s. 46. Where a constable has reasonable cause to believe that a child would be otherwise likely to suffer significant harm, he or she may remove the child to 'suitable accommodation'. Alternatively, such steps as are reasonable may be taken to ensure that the child's removal from hospital, or other place in which the child is being accommodated, is prevented. When these powers are exercised, the child is said to be in 'police protection' (s. 46(2)). No child can be kept in police protection for more than seventy-two hours (s. 46(6)).

PROTECTING CHILDREN BY PRIVATE ORDERS

Can a local authority protect an abused child or one at risk of abuse by using the private law orders in Part II of the Children Act? The Act is quite clear. Section 9(2) states: 'No application may be made by a local authority for a residence order or contact order and no court shall make such an order in favour of a local authority.' And subs. 5 of the same section directs that 'no court shall exercise its powers to make a specific issue order or prohibited steps order – (a) with a view to achieving a result which could be achieved by making a residence order or contact order'. The rationale is clear: if a local authority were able to acquire a residence order, it would have parental responsibility vested in it and would be able to determine where the child lived without satisfying the minimum threshold conditions for a care order; if a local authority could acquire a contact order, it would acquire rights and powers similar to those it would get with a supervision order, again without satisfying the hurdle of s. 31(2). Section 9(5) is designed to prevent local authorities achieving these ends through the back door.[112]

In *Nottingham CC* v. *P*[113] these provisions were tested. The local authority wanted the court to order that the father should not reside in the same household as his daughters and should not have any contact with them unless they themselves wished to have contact with him, and that any such contact should be supervised by the social services department. It stated that it was making the application to stop/prevent the sexual abuse of the daughters by the father and its emotionally and physically damaging effects. It applied for a prohibited steps order. As Sir Stephen Brown P put it in the Court of Appeal, the case raised 'important questions of law and policy concerning the power of a local authority to seek to make use of the private law provisions ... in Part II of the Children Act 1989 instead of proceeding by way of the public law provisions contained in Part IV of the ... Act'.[114] Despite the fact that the local authority had earlier obtained emergency protection orders (and thus had to satisfy the 'significant harm' test) and notwithstanding a s. 37 reference, the authority refused to apply under s. 31, most obviously for a supervision order. The attitude of Nottingham County Council was not unique. As Ward J, at first instance, observed, 'a climate of co-operation and of partnership is more easily able to exist if the menu of practical solutions is offered to the unhappy parents rather than that emotive matters of care and supervision are imposed upon them'.[115]

The Court of Appeal held that it could not make a prohibited steps order. On the wider question of policy, Sir Stephen Brown P said:

> We consider that this court should make it clear that the route chosen by the local authority in this case was wholly inappropriate. In cases where children are found to be at risk of suffering significant harm within the meaning of s. 31 of the Children Act 1989, a clear duty arises on the part of local authorities to take steps to protect them. In such circumstances, a local authority is required to assume responsibility and to intervene in the family arrangements in order to protect the child or children. Part IV specifically provides them with wide powers and wide discretion. The Act envisages that local authorities may place children with their parents even though they have a care order under s. 31. A supervision order may be viewed as being less Draconian but it gives the local authorities a wide discretion as to how to deal with children and with the family ... A prohibited steps order ... could not in any circumstances be regarded as providing a substitute for an order under Part IV of the Children Act 1989.

> Furthermore, it is very doubtful indeed whether a prohibited steps order could in any circumstances be used to 'oust' a father from a matrimonial home.[116]

And later in his judgment he expressed the deep concern of the court 'at the absence of any power to direct [the] authority to take steps to protect the children', noting that in the former wardship jurisdiction it might well have been able to do so.[117]

Even if the court were able in these circumstances to grant a prohibited steps order, it is difficult to see what it would achieve. A prohibited steps order would not confer on the local authority any direct power to protect the children.

Ward J had sought an imaginative solution. He made a residence order in favour of the mother, conditional (see s. 11(7)) upon the father removing himself from the home and not re-entering until permitted to do so by the court. The Court of Appeal thought this solution artificial and allowed appeals against the residence order, but it desisted from commenting upon Ward J's use of s. 11. The question is therefore still open as to whether an ouster condition can be attached to a residence order. Parliament rejected a clause that would have countenanced ouster.[118] There are real problems here. If ouster is to be allowed, for how long should it last? For as long as an emergency protection order (a maximum of fifteen days), three months, 'until further order'?[119] And what should the criteria for ouster be? To invoke the paramountcy principle would be to turn the clock back to before *Richards* v. *Richards*,[120] but the Court of Appeal has already denied[121] that s. 1(1) has any effect on the Lord's ruling in that case. Surely, the Matrimonial Homes Act 1983 criteria (in s. 1(3) of that Act) can have no relevance – or can they? They refer, after all, to conduct, and there was little doubt as to the husband/father's misconduct in *Nottingham CC* v. *P*.

Had the Nottingham decision been upheld, there would also have been some odd consequences. The local authority would have been expected to supervise contact even though it had deliberately desisted from applying for a supervision order. Furthermore, it would seem that a court could make such a direction even though no one applied for it (see

s. 10(1)(b)). In *Leeds County Council* v. C[122] Booth J rejected the idea that s. 11(7) could be used to make a local authority supervise contact, pointing to s. 16 and the family assistance order.[123] But the Leeds case was not cited in *Nottinghamshire*. There are thus conflicting views as to the scope of s. 11(7), both at first instance. Booth J's is undoubtedly closer to the text of the Children Act, but perhaps Ward J's is closer to its spirit. Debates on the use and scope of private law remedies in the battle to conquer child abuse are set to rage, presumably until there is further statutory intervention and clarification.[124]

REFERENCES

1. (London, HMSO, 1991), para. 6.40.
2. See s. 31(2).
3. This article ignores criminal law responses to child abuse.
4. Lord Mackay, 'Joseph Jackson Memorial Lecture', 139 NLJ 505, 508 (1989).
5. The only 'authorised person' (see s. 31(1), (9)).
6. See s. 1(5) and *Humberside CC* v. *B* [1993] 1 FLR 257.
7. There is a most useful series of articles on this in *Community Care*, 28 October 1993.
8. See s. 2 and J. Eekelaar (1991) JSWL 37.
9. See s. 44.
10. See s. 43.
11. Under s. 37. See *Re H* [1993] 2 FCR 277: the provision is to be widely construed.
12. Particularly in the light of the *Nottinghamshire CC* v. *P* litigation, discussed below.
13. As defined in s. 10.
14. But note the refusal of the Court of Appeal to interpret s. 1(1) of the Children Act as overruling *Richards* v. *Richards* [1984] AC 174 (see *Gibson* v. *Austin* [1992] 2 FLR 437).
15. See s. 8. But a local authority may not apply for, or be granted, a residence order (see s. 9(2)).
16. See *Re D* [1977] Fam 158; *Re R* [1987] 2 FLR 400.
17. By s. 100. But see *Re DB and CB* [1993] 2 FLR which may herald a move back by the courts towards encouraging local authorities to invoke inherent jurisdiction.
18. See S. M. Cretney in D. Freestone (ed.), *Children and the Law* (Hull University Press, 1990), and M. Freeman, *Current Legal Problems* (1992).
19. See vol. 1, para. 3.12.
20. See, further, M. Freeman in D. Freestone (ed.), *op. cit.* (n. 18), and M. Freeman,

Children, Their Families and the Law (Basingstoke, Macmillan, 1992), pp. 99–112.

21. (London, HMSO, 1985), para. 15(15).
22. *Op. cit.* (n. 19), para. 3.19. Cf. J. Goldstein, A. Freud and A. Solnit, *Before the Best Interests of the Child* (New York, Free Press, 1979), p. 72; on which see M. Freeman, *The Rights and Wrongs of Children* (London, Pinter, 1988), pp. 253–5.
23. *Op. cit.* (n. 19), para. 3.19.
24. *Idem.*
25. *Re B* [1990] 2 FLR 317.
26. M. Woodhead in A. James and A. Prout (eds), *Constructing and Reconstructing Childhood* (London, Falmer Press, 1990), p. 73.
27. See J. Korbin, *Child Abuse and Neglect* (Berkeley, University of California Press, 1981).
28. Prohibition of Female Circumcision Act 1985.
29. See P. Newell, *The UN Convention and Children's Rights in the UK* (London, National Children's Bureau, 1991), pp. 96–7, and A. Miller, *Banished Knowledge* (London, Virago Press, 1991), pp. 136–8. See, further, D. Finkelhor and J. Korbin (1988)12 Child Abuse and Neglect 3.
30. See M. Freeman, *Violence in the Home: A Socio-Legal Study* (Aldershot, Gower Press, 1979), pp. 31–2; A. Miller, *For Your Own Good* (London, Virago Press, 1987).
31. Austria's Supreme Court had to interpret this ban in a child custody dispute in 1993. See M. Freeman 1 IJCR (1993).
32. *Hansard*, HL vol. 503, col. 342.
33. See his article in 181 J. American Medical Association 17 (1962). See, further, N. Parton (1979)9 British Journal of Social Work 431.
34. See M. Freeman in M. Partington and J. Jowell, *Welfare Law and Policy* (London, Pinter, 1979), p. 223.
35. *Op. cit.* (n. 19), para. 3.19.
36. *Op. cit.* (n. 1), para. 6.40.
37. *F v. Suffolk CC* (1981)2 FLR 208.
38. See S. Wolkind (1988) JSWL 82.
39. [1988] 1 FLR 462.
40. Cf. B. Campbell, *Unofficial Secrets* (London, Virago, 1988) with S. Bell, *When Salem Came to the 'Boro* (London, Pan, 1988). See, further, M. Freeman (1989) 42 CLP 85.
41. See D. Finkelhor, *Child Sexual Abuse* (London, Sage, 1984); J. Haugaard and N. Reppucci, *The Sexual Abuse of Children* (San Francisco, Jossey Bass); K. Faller, *Child Sexual Abuse* (New York, Columbia University Press, 1988). Also very useful is ch. 5 of M. King and J. Trowell, *Children's Welfare and the Law* (London, Sage, 1992).
42. *Re W* [1987] 1 FLR 297; *Re G* [1988] 1 FLR 314; *Re H*; *Re K* [1989] 2 FLR 313.
43. Or possibly ill-treatment, depending on the circumstances.
44. *R v. Hopley* (1860)2 F and F 202.
45. *Idem.*

46. Although babies were, it seems, removed from mothers at birth despite this restriction. See M. Freeman (1980) 10 Family Law 131.
47. *Re H* [1993] 2 FLR 541.
48. *Ibid.*, p. 548.
49. *Re M* [1988] Adoption and Fostering 49.
50. [1993] 1 FLR 281.
51. *Ibid.*, p. 288.
52. *Ibid.*, p. 289. See also Thorpe J in *Re A* [1993] 1 FLR 824, 826.
53. [1987] AC 317.
54. *Ibid.*, p. 350A.
55. *Ibid.*, p. 346E.
56. [1993] 1 FLR 554.
57. *Ibid.*, p. 557A.
58. [1993] 1 FLR 815.
59. [1985] FLR 325.
60. *Op. cit.* (n. 58), p. 818.
61. And cf. *H* v. *Sheffield CC* (1981) JSWL 303.
62. *The Times*, 20 October 1993.
63. *Hansard*, HL vol. 503, col. 354.
64. Vol. 1, para. 3.20.
65. As an example, there is evidence that mothers of Down's Syndrome children suffer disproportionately from depression, so that the birth of a Down's Syndrome child can turn a moderately successful or shaky marriage into a poor or dysfunctional one, with obvious effect on the child's development and health. See A. Gath, *Down's Syndrome and the Family: The Early Years* (London, Academic Press, 1978).
66. Because it is thought that such cases should be made the subject of education supervision orders under s. 36 (as amended by the Education Act 1993).
67. [1992] 2 FLR 7.
68. 'Beyond parental control' questions are outside the remit of this article, and are not discussed.
69. See *Guidance*, vol. 1, para. 3.23.
70. [1993] 1 FLR 815.
71. *Hansard*, HL vol. 512, col. 756 *per* Lord Mackay.
72. A pre-Act illustration is *Re P* [1988] 1 FLR 328.
73. Under part II of the Act.
74. *Children: The New Law* (Bristol, Family Law, 1990), p. 101.
75. See for example s. 22(5)(c), schedule 2, para. 11 and principle 21 of *Principles and Practice in Regulations and Guidance*. See also S. Macdonald, *All Equal under the Act?* (London, National Institute of Social Work, 1991).
76. [1987] 2 FLR 12.
77. In D. Freestone (ed.), *op. cit.* (n. 20), at pp. 149–50.
78. [1993] 1 FLR 815.
79. *Op. cit.* (n. 19).
80. [1993] 1 FLR 257.

81. [1993] 1 FLR 866.
82. [1993] 1 FLR 554.
83. [1993] 1 FLR 308.
84. *Ibid.*, p. 309.
85. *Per* Lord MacDermott in *J* v *C* [1970] AC 668.
86. [1993] 1 FLR 883.
87. *Ibid.*, p. 899 *per* Evans LJ.
88. *M* v. *M* [1973] 2 All ER 81.
89. *Op. cit.* (n. 86), p. 897.
90. [1971] 3 All ER 682 where the denial of access to a parent was described as a 'Draconian order'.
91. *Per* Dunn J in *Re D* [1977] Fam 157.
92. Of which wardship is merely a species. But there is no difference between the powers under the High Court's inherent jurisdiction and its powers in wardship. See *Re J* [1992] 2 FLR 165. See also *Re O* [1993] 2 FLR 149.
93. See N. Lowe's criticism in (1989) 139 NLJ 87.
94. In *Re DB and CB* [1993] 2 FLR.
95. *South Glamorgan CC* v. *W and B* [1993]1 FLR 574.
96. *Ibid.*, p. 584.
97. Under s. 38(6).
98. *Op. cit.* (n. 95).
99. [1991] 4 All ER 177 (a psychotic 15-year-old girl).
100. [1992] 4 All ER 627 (anorexia nervosa).
101. [1986] AC 112.
102. See M. Freeman (1993) 17 Adoption and Fostering 14.
103. This now exists in much of the common law world, following the US lead, and in several European countries. Its introduction was recently recommended in New Zealand. The *Review of Child Care Law* came out against introducing this in England (see para. 12(4)).
104. Section 47 also attempts to promote inter-agency cooperation (see s. 47(9)–(11)).
105. Vol. 1, para. 4.9.
106. *Ibid.*, para. 4.4.
107. *Ibid.*, para. 4.12.
108. See the Cleveland Report: Dame E. Butler-Sloss, *Report of the Inquiry into Child Abuse in Cleveland (1987)*, Cm 412 (London, HMSO, 1988), para. 16.5.
109. Vol. 1, para. 4.30.
110. Although ouster orders usually only last for three months (*Practice Note* [1978] 2 All ER 1056), they may be 'until further order' (*Galan* v. *Galan* [1985] FLR 905).
111. This is recognised in *Working Together* (see paras. 4.11–4.17).
112. Acknowledged by Ward J in *Nottinghamshire CC* v. *P* [1993] 1 FLR 514, 539 and by the Court of Appeal ([1993] 2 FLR 134, 143).
113. [1993] 2 FLR 134.
114. *Ibid.*, p. 136.
115. [1993] 1 FLR 514, 539.

116. *Op. cit.* (n. 113), p. 143–4.
117. *Ibid.*, p. 148.
118. See *Hansard*, HC 27 October 1989.
119. Cf. *Galan* v. *Galan* [1985] FLR 905.
120. [1984] AC 174.
121. In *Gibson* v. *Austin* [1992] 2 FLR 437.
122. [1993] 1 FLR 269.
123. Although there are limits on this, notably a time limit of six months.
124. One such debate took place between Patricia Scotland QC and David White, the Director of Nottinghamshire Social Services, at the Social Services Conference in Solihull in October 1993 (see *Community Care*, 4 November 1993, p. 5). See also N. Lowe, 5 Journal of Child Law 105 (1993), and H. Barnett, 23 Family Law 591 (1993).

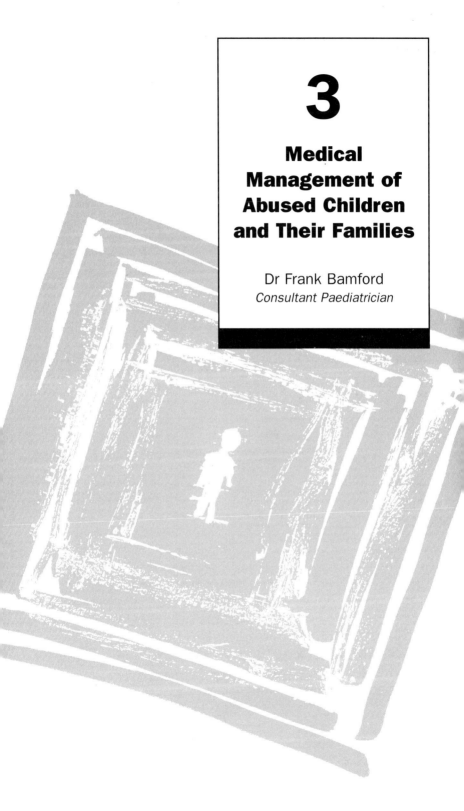

3

Medical Management of Abused Children and Their Families

Dr Frank Bamford
Consultant Paediatrician

The Hippocratic dictum *primum non nocere* – first do no harm – applies to all medical practice, not least to that connected with child abuse. Harm to abused children is not restricted to the direct effect of actions or default of care by their parents. It can be caused by the process of protecting them. Harm attributable to delays in legal proceedings is now well recognised. In the medical management of abused children there is a potential for damage in several respects, including that arising from wrong diagnosis, unnecessarily repetitive examinations and by impairment of trust in essential services.

Wrong Diagnosis

There is a common presumption that faulty diagnosis leads only to an injustice to parents because their children are wrongly diagnosed as having been abused when, in fact, there has been no abuse, but it is important to remember that there are two sides to the coin. Failure to diagnose can have disastrous consequences for children and, unlike their parents, they are often too young or too frightened to object to the error and are left defenceless. We walk along a tightrope and inevitably there will be occasions when, even if the greatest care and skill have been employed, falls to one side or the other will occur.

The falsely accused parent deserves great sympathy but this has to be balanced against the knowledge that excessive caution in diagnosis can leave children in grave danger. In the event of failure to diagnose there is not only a likelihood of continued suffering but also a significant risk that future injuries will escalate in severity, causing death or permanent disability and, in particular, brain injury. The tendency for successive injuries to escalate in severity has been known for many years. For example, in an early study from Birmingham of 134 children, 21 died and 7 of them were known to have been battered more than once; 6 others had a sibling who had been battered and 10 of the 113 children who survived battering had a deceased sibling.[1]

REPEATED EXAMINATION

It is often necessary for an abused child to be examined more than once because there is a need to ensure that injuries have resolved or that treatment has been effective. Since diagnosis is usually an opinion not susceptible to proof by objective biological tests, the second opinion of an experienced colleague is often helpful and requesting the opinion is simply prudent, good practice. Examinations of children should be *for* children, and subjecting them to several examinations for purposes other than their medical welfare is questionable.

The potential for harm by re-examination is greatest in cases of suspected child sexual abuse. Ideally, the initial examination should be the commencement of a healing process; a time when reassurance is given about integrity and subsequent normality. It should not be undermined by doubts that are, almost inevitably, introduced by a second examination. Furthermore, if a child has been abused, repeated examination may be seen as another intrusion, i.e. repeated abuse.

The *Report of the Inquiry into Child Abuse in Cleveland*[2] recognised that medical examination for forensic or other evidential purposes unconnected with the immediate care of the child posed difficult problems. It recommended that the consent of parents should be sought but, in practice, most re-examinations are requested by parents who do not believe the initial examiner and they are very unlikely to object to the request of a guardian ad litem who has similar doubts. Parental consent does not make the process any less traumatic for the child and there should be an attempt to reach agreement on medical issues, if possible, without further examination.

IMPAIRED CONFIDENCE IN ESSENTIAL SERVICES

It is understandable that parents may be reluctant to return with their child to a hospital at which abuse of the child was diagnosed. In urban conurbations a return to the same hospital can usually be avoided but delay or reluctance to attend in the case of medical need when there is no alternative service could imperil the health or life of the child. Fortunately it does not seem to be a frequent problem but clearly there is a duty to avoid alienation of parents as much as is consistent with the welfare of their child. Medical diagnosis of abuse is primarily a service for the child but it can also be sensibly viewed as a service for parents.

Parents feel threatened when arbitrary decisions are made and when blame is implied. Avoiding them is a matter of experience. Experience also teaches that the best way to defuse tense situations which sometimes arise is to proceed calmly with a medical history as in any other consultation. The discipline involved is immediately recognised by most parents and it has the advantage of methodically eliciting information of considerable importance in the evaluation of the family. A history of emotional development is very valuable and asking about illnesses in the family often gives the parent an opportunity to talk about their problems. Abusing parents will often spend more time talking about themselves than about their children. Of course, the history must be recorded in detail, as must the clinical findings.

ABUSE BY FALSE COMPLAINT

Separated parents often complain about the care given by the other parent during contact visits. Occasionally they use the complaints to manipulate or suspend contact. Legitimate health problems may be exaggerated by parents and some illnesses, especially those with psychosomatic components, may be exacerbated by the inherent stress. It is important for those giving medical opinions to actually see what happens because accounts of illness in these circumstances can be untrustworthy.

More sinister are complaints by one parent that the child has been sexually abused by the other parent or by his or her new partner. They seem to have increased in frequency in the past few years. Once the complaint has been made it is almost certain that the child has been abused one way or another. Either there has been sexual abuse or there has been an attempt to use the child for the purposes of the adult.

The medical examiner is more or less obliged to examine the child and to refer the matter for enquiry under the child protection procedures. If the child has not been sexually abused, he or she becomes the vehicle of the alternative form of abuse and nothing is more likely to strain his or her relationship with the complaining parent.

DIFFERENTIAL DIAGNOSIS

A careful consideration of alternative explanations for clinical findings indicative of injury is mandatory. The possibilities vary with the circumstances of the particular case. Osteogenesis imperfecta is now well known to the courts and to various professions dealing with abused children. Dr Wynne dealt with the condition in a previous edition of this book.[3] There are other metabolic bone disorders in which precise diagnosis is uncertain and I have no doubt that new disorders affecting bone strength have still to be discovered. There is room for honest doubt and a need for careful, methodical enquiry but this has to be set against the risk of causing confusion in cases where children need protection.

The same principles apply with respect to other types of injury and an obscure differential diagnosis can be constructed for almost all of them. Two spurious explanations used commonly are head-banging, to explain intracranial injury, and 'he's like me – he bruises easily'. There are others, but these two are discussed below.

HEAD-BANGING

Head-banging consists of a voluntary, repetitive banging of the head against head boards, cot railings or other objects. It is common, occurring in approximately one in twenty children. Usually it commences between 6 and 10 months of age and continues until 2½ to 3 years. It occurs most frequently prior to sleep or when the child is tired or upset.

Affected children usually rock to and fro on their hands and knees, banging the centre of their foreheads. Some sit using their arms to push themselves, and others lie face down raising their head and then letting it drop onto a pillow. The most violent forms usually occur with the child kneeling or standing, and holding the cot rail while hitting their foreheads. A few lie on their backs, rocking and banging their temples.

The frequency of banging varies but is usually about forty times per minute and it goes on for considerable periods, often in excess of an hour. Children do not seem to suffer pain while head-banging and the majority do not cry. They may cause small bruises or abrasions over their foreheads or at the back of their skulls. These are most commonly seen in mentally handicapped children. Intracranial injury from head-banging has not been recorded and there is a statement in the medical literature that 'no evidence of acquired injury to the brain has been noted clinically or on E.E.G.'.[4]

The cause of head-banging is unknown and there are probably several different contributory factors. In some cases it is associated with rearing in isolation and with stress and depression. There is also a greater frequency in children who live in institutions and in those who are mentally handicapped. Persistence into later childhood may occur in the latter groups.

'HE BRUISES EASILY'

Bruises are infiltrations of blood in tissues under the skin. They are usually caused by blunt trauma, when they are often associated with swelling, or by pressure. In the context of child abuse, small, round, flat bruises are common. Bruises may also be caused by shearing forces acting on the skin or by negative pressure produced by sucking or by blood vessel damage due to local inflammatory disease or atrophy of surrounding tissues as in the ano-genital skin disorder, lichen sclerosus et atrophicus. Bruising may also be a manifestation of septicaemia or of various blood disorders. It is the possibility of the latter that is sometimes used to mitigate or explain bruising in cases of non-accidental injury. A problem for paediatricians is to decide whether tests for these disorders are necessary in all cases.

All children get bruises. Unexplained accidental bruises are uncommon before infants become independently mobile but during the second year of life the number increases greatly and by 3 to 4 years children do not have less than three bruises at any one time.[5] In a review of children, partly at a child welfare clinic and partly at a day nursery, we found that 25 per cent had five bruises and another 25 per cent had six bruises. None had seven or more bruises. Half of the bruises were on the legs and only a quarter on the head, whereas 60 per cent of non-accidental bruising is on the head.[6]

The numbers of bruises and their distribution help to distinguish accidental from non-accidental injury and certain patterns of bruising can also be recognised – for example, finger-tip bruising of a very firm grip, the mark of a slap across the face, bruising caused by bites, tram-line bruises produced by a rod and the J-shaped mark of a whip. All of these can be recognised with reasonable confidence and only in the event of excessive size would a bleeding disorder be a significant possibility.

It is not necessary for all children who have been non-accidentally injured to have blood taken to test for these disorders, but the slightest suspicion derived from a family medical history should trigger testing, especially in male children because some of the coagulation disorders are inherited by them through their unaffected mothers. It is also prudent to arrange for tests whenever there is a complaint that 'he bruises easily', although in the majority of cases no abnormality will be found.

Blood coagulation is a complex process. If it is faulty at any stage, the affected person is likely to bleed or to bruise abnormally. Generally, bruises are much larger than normal rather than more numerous, and they are less likely to form a recognisable pattern.

When a blood vessel is broken, the first stage in controlling blood loss is constriction of the vessel, followed by formation of a plug of platelet cells from the blood. Clearly there will be excessive bleeding or bruising if there are insufficient numbers of platelet cells or if they do not have the adhesive property that enables them to stick together. The latter may be influenced by the consumption of aspirin, and other drugs can affect platelet numbers and function, so a detailed history of any recent medication is important.

The next stage of coagulation involves the interaction of several coagulation factors. They are factors 8, 9, 11 and 12, referred to as intrinsic factors, and they are activated during coagulation. The extrinsic pathway consists of factor 7 which is converted to an activated form and the two groups of factors interact, forming further coagulation factors. These enable a substance called prothrombin from the liver to be converted to thrombin and this in turn enables the conversion of another substance called fibrinogen to fibrin which stabilises the platelet plug.

The complexity of this process will be appreciated from the greatly over-simplified account above and it will be clear that disorders of the liver or a congenital absence of one of the coagulation factors will lead to failure of stable clot formation. Fortunately, each stage in the process does not need to be tested whenever there is a suspicion of easy bruising. There are screening tests which are used to exclude defects in different groups of disorders, and only in the case of a screening test being positive are further detailed analyses required.

The screening tests employed may vary slightly in different laboratories but the following are widely used:

1. A platelet count – the normal range is between 150 and 400 $\times$ 10^9–/1. If the count falls below 40×10^9–/1, bleeding or spontaneous bruising is likely to occur.

2. Bleeding time – tests the capacity of the blood vessel to constrict and the function of platelet cells.

3. Activated partial thromboplastin time (APTT) – tests the coagulation factors in the intrinsic pathway and their interaction.

4. Prothrombin time (PT) – tests the extrinsic pathway.

5. Fibrin degradation products and/or thrombin clotting time (TCT) is provided by some laboratories and detects abnormalities of fibrinogen.

Platelet counts, APPT and PT are the most important in the context of child abuse, and in criminal proceedings dependent on evidence of bruising they would be a minimum requirement.

MONGOLIAN BLUE SPOTS AND HAEMANGIOMATA

Occasional mistakes have occurred in the recognition of bruises. Young children from pigmented races and those of mixed race often have blue coloured areas on their backs that look similar to bruises. They are usually over the lower part of the back but they are seen occasionally elsewhere on the back or shoulders. The uninitiated may mistake them for bruises, the distinction being that the colour tends to be uniform, does not change within a few days and is not associated with other signs of trauma such as swelling or abrasions.

Haemangiomata are collections of anomalous blood vessels. Some of them appear a few weeks after birth. Most superficial haemangiomata are easily recognisable either as a slightly raised, bright red area (strawberry haemangioma) or as a flat, irregular, purple patch, often on the skin of the face (port wine stain). Occasionally haemangiomata involving deeper blood vessels are seen on the surface only as a slightly blue colour of the skin. A significant proportion of them occur between the anus and genitalia and they can be mistaken for bruises by the unwary.

MUNCHAUSEN SYNDROME BY PROXY

Different forms of child abuse assume a prominence for a period before they are superseded by other aspects of the problem. During the 1980s child sexual abuse was a predominant issue and the fashion for the 1990s looks like being Munchausen Syndrome by Proxy. It is important to remember that there is considerable overlap between all forms of abuse.

The *Adventures of Baron Munchausen* is a series of extravagant stories about a soldier and adventurer who lived in Northern Germany in the eighteenth century.[7] They are told with very precise detail. In 1951 Asher, a London physician, described patients who told false and exaggerated stories, usually to get themselves accommodated in hospitals. He called their condition Munchausen Syndrome in memory of the famous baron. Meadow perceived that some mothers used their children to get attention from medical personnel and he coined the term 'Munchausen Syndrome by Proxy' in 1977 (see Chapter 7).

Like many other conditions it is a spectrum, from something fairly innocuous at one end to something extremely dangerous at the other. It may be no more than the extreme anxiety of an inexperienced, lonely mother. She takes her child to the doctor frequently and as a consequence the child is exposed to repeated examinations, maybe investigations and often unnecessary treatment. The abuser is not the mother but the doctor.

Midway across the spectrum are mothers who not only make false complaints about symptoms in their children, but also reinforce them by tampering with specimens – for example, by adding their own blood to samples of urine or by heating thermometers, etc. After a time they are found out because somebody sees them doing it or blood groups in specimens are checked when suspicion arises. In many cases the harm to the child is confined to the discomfort of unnecessary investigations and the inconvenience of prolonged hospitalisation, but in some cases the process acquires a momentum of its own, the mother becomes too involved or frightened to call a halt and the child is subject to serious and potentially hazardous procedures such as intravenous feeding or surgical operations. Clearly there is no single method of management that is universally applicable but there is a need in all cases to bring the matter out into the open.

At the far end of the spectrum are those mothers who actually fabricate illness in their children. It is a phenomenon that is extremely dangerous, often involving suffocation or partial suffocation of the child. The term now used is 'imposed upper airway obstruction' but I do not think that there is any merit in dressing up the word 'suffocation' which is understood by everybody. Many lay people cannot believe or understand that it happens but, nevertheless, its occurrence in some cases is beyond doubt and some children die or are left with severe anoxic brain damage.

Of those who die, some are registered as cot deaths. This was drawn to attention by Emery, who used the phrase 'the gently battered child'.[8] Cot death is an unsatisfactory term describing a place and implying a mode of death but there are many different causes for cot death and suffocation is one of them. This possibility and the increasing public awareness of it can be a source of distress to those parents – the majority – who lose children by cot death due to natural phenomena. The two groups need to be distinguished.

Children who are being suffocated are usually brought for attention with a complaint that they are having recurrent episodes of stopping breathing, i.e. recurrent apnoea attacks. These are not uncommon in paediatric practice and there are several causes for them. Polygraph recording devices can be used to identify the probable cause and a specific type of trace is seen in those cases when breathing is obstructed. Unfortunately, they are not absolutely reliable or specific to imposed obstruction but they are, nevertheless, valuable.

Definitive diagnosis requires either that mothers say what they have done, which is very unusual unless they are confronted with some evidence of it, or that they are seen suffocating their child. Chance observation in a hospital ward is unlikely although affected mothers persist with their activities after admission even to the point of causing serious injury. Observation is inevitably incomplete and they manage to obstruct their child's airway during unobserved moments. They then call for assistance and nursing staff find the child collapsed, pale or blue and often with a reduced heart rate. There is convincing evidence of asphyxiation but the crucial point of the history in these cases is that only the mother is ever present at the onset of an attack. If anybody other than her genuinely sees the onset of apnoea, it more or less excludes the possibility of abusive suffocation.

When there are substantial reasons for believing that a child is being suffocated, usually when there is evidence of obstructive apnoea and only the mother is present at the onset of attacks, proof of diagnosis can be obtained by covert video surveillance. There are a number of problems. First, there can be technical problems, such as the mother getting between the camera and the baby during the episode. This is usually overcome by using two cameras. The film may show the mother with her hand in proximity to her baby's nose or mouth but the quality of the film may be insufficient to be sure that respiration had been obstructed. This is inferred from concurrent polygraph tracings and by the sound of the baby struggling to breathe. The second problem is that it is a deception which undermines the trust that is essential to any therapeutic relationship, and third, it is an invasion of the parent's privacy. There is an ethical dilemma but the practice can be justified on the basis that there is a general public acceptance of the use of covert video surveillance for the protection of property and, when there is a likelihood of child abuse, there is a strong positive balance between the good to be achieved by the prevention of death, disability or suffering and the harm to be done by intruding on the rights of the parent.

The likelihood of continuing abuse in cases of Munchausen Syndrome by Proxy is documented. Children from fifty-six families who had been victims of fabricated illness were described.[9] It was found that 64 per cent of them had suffered more than one illness fabricated by their mothers. Many (73 per cent) had had additional problems such as non-accidental injury (29 per cent) and failure to thrive (29 per cent). A sinister aspect of the findings was that 11 per cent had a sibling who had died in early childhood without an identified cause of death. Many siblings of index children had fared badly, 39 per cent had suffered an illness fabricated by their mothers and 17 per cent had been affected either by failure to thrive, non-accidental injury, inappropriate medication or neglect.

MISUSE OF DRUGS

In Munchausen Syndrome by Proxy, drugs are sometimes prescribed inappropriately because of the false history or fabricated clinical signs.

Occasionally these drugs are given in excessive dosage or drugs prescribed for parents are given to children. The drugs most commonly
identified are those with sedative properties and they are usually found
in urine samples sent for toxicology screening tests, but many different
types of substance may be given including insulin, excessive salt and cor-
rosive compounds such as caustic soda crystals, and not all of them are
easily tracked down.

Of contemporary importance are drugs of addiction and compounds
such as methadone, used to treat heroin addiction. Paediatricians are
now familiar with withdrawal effects in newborn babies of addicted
mothers. Later administration of the drugs to children has been relatively uncommon in Britain so far but there have been some deaths. Deaths
may occur because of non-accidental injury by a parent under the influence of drugs while in charge of the child or, more commonly, by children obtaining or being given drugs in doses sufficient to cause respira-
tory depression. Accidental poisoning is common in children between 1
and 4 years old and within these age groups they are quite likely to take
methadone or other drugs that are left around. Distinguishing between
accidental poisoning and that due to administered drugs may be impossible but the identification of drugs in a child under 1 year old should
raise strong suspicion.

PREDICTION AND PREVENTION OF CHILD ABUSE – AN EMPTY HOPE?

Simply providing extra support for families does not necessarily influence poor patterns of parenting and no immediate effect on the occurrence of child abuse is to be expected.[10] Child abuse is rarely a simple
matter. Its causes are usually multifactorial and there is great variety in
the nature of injuries that are produced. Not only do single acts of abuse
have many causes but they may also have several different effects. For
example, whether a child struck across the face gets away with a hand-
print bruise or sustains a major haemorrhage within the skull may
depend more on luck than on the parents' feelings about him or her. The

significance of harm is not always in direct proportion to the severity of injury.

It is during the childhood of the abusing parent that the seeds of future child abuse are sown and it is the rescue of children from abuse and deprivation now that will help to prevent child abuse in the next generation. Care of parents later in their lives, before the birth of their children, may also be important. Prevention has to do with the quality of care received by a mother during pregnancy, her experience of labour and most importantly the way in which she and her baby are treated at birth. It has to do with the careful and humane management of sick and premature infants and especially with the support and help given to the parents who have abnormal or disappointing children. It has to do with the mother's satisfaction in nurturing her child and her understanding and assurance about minor anomalies of behaviour. It has to do with the support and help that she receives during the universal infectious illnesses of childhood and it may have to do with the recognition of early signs of abuse and intervention before things get too bad. The prevention of all or even most child abuse may be a forlorn hope but it ought to be susceptible to reduction in the long term.

REFERENCES

1. S. M. Smith and R. Hanson, '134 Battered Children: A medical and psychological study', *British Medical Journal* (1974), ii, 666–70.
2. Dame E. Butler-Sloss, *Report of the Inquiry into Child Abuse in Cleveland (1987)*, Cm 412, (London, HMSO, 1988).
3. J. Wynne, 'Medical Aspects of Child Abuse', in A. Levy (ed.), *Focus on Child Abuse* (London, Hawksmere, 1989).
4. H. Kravitz, V. Rosenthal, Z. Teplitz, J. B. Murphy and R. E. Lesser, 'A Study of Head-Banging in Infants and Children', *Diseases of the Nervous System* (1969), 21, 203–8.
5. J. H. Keen, 'Normal Bruises in Pre-school Children', *Archives of Disease in Childhood* (L) (1981), pp. 56, 75.
6. D. M. Roberton, P. Barbor and D. Hull, 'Unusual Injury? Recent injury in normal children and children with suspected non-accidental injury', *British Medical Journal* (1982), 285, ii, 1399–401.

7. R. E. Raspe, *et al., The Adventures of Baron Munchausen*, (London, Harrap, 1985).
8. E. M. Taylor and J. L. Emery, 'Two Year Study of the Causes of Post-neonatal Deaths Classified in Terms of Preventability', *Archives of Disease in Childhood* (1982), 57, 668–73.
9. C. N. Bools, B. A. Neale and S. R. Meadow, 'Co-morbidity Associated with Fabricated Illness (Munchausen Syndrome by Proxy)', *Archives of Disease in Childhood* (1992), 67, 77–9.
10. G. T. Lealman, D. Haigh, J. M. Philips, J. Stone and C. Ord-Smith, 'Prediction and Prevention of Child Abuse: – An empty hope', *Lancet* (1983), i, 1423–4.

4

Child Sexual Abuse, Family Life and the Children Act

Margery Bray
Social Work Consultant

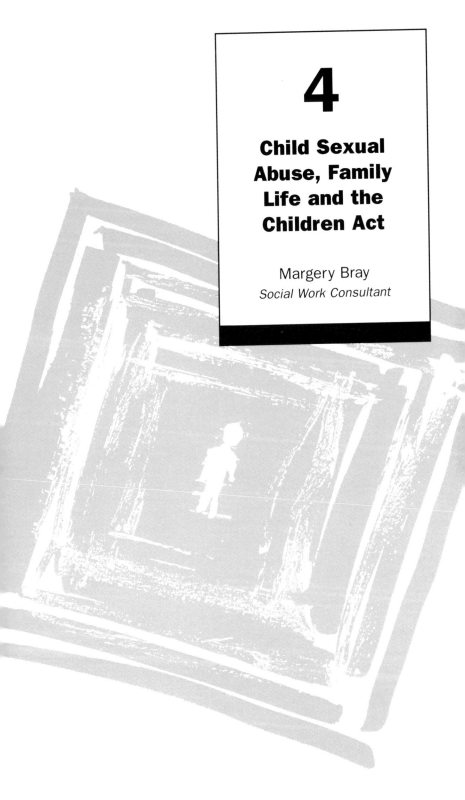

The venue is the House of Commons, the context a debate on children, and the date 25 June 1993. At 12.10pm Mr Fabricant (Mid-Staffordshire) rises to address the House on the Children Act. Pausing momentarily to explain how a recent eye injury has resulted in the presence of his Dame Edna Everage face furniture, he reveals that he has had to make the difficult choice of 'looking like Roy Orbison or wearing an eye patch and looking like Moshe Dayan'. He has opted for the Roy Orbison look. Moving on from the subject of his personal appearance, Mr Fabricant shifts his (now doubtless richly enhanced) focus to the Children Act. He goes on to address the House:

> I believe that it was Oscar Wilde who said that the best way to make children was to make them happy. I could not agree more. The good health, well-being and happiness of children should not only be the aim of parents everywhere but should be the responsibility of Government. It is our responsibility that the present Government have taken on with relish; they have recognised the duty of care and are fulfilling their obligation. We are witnessing a marked improvement in the health of children as many Honourable members have said. The Children Act 1989, on which I shall concentrate today, was one of the most comprehensive and radical reforms of child law enacted by Parliament for many years. The Act has been widely hailed as a great success.
>
> The opposition – notably the Right Honourable Member for Islwyn (Mr Kinnock) – have for many years scorned what they call our obsession with the traditional family or with family values. We make no apology for that so-called obsession – we are not embarrassed by it. I believe that it is family values that maintain this structure of society and protect children in our society. Even Professor Halsey, for so long a Labour Party guru and a major influence on the Labour Party's thinking on social issues, last year extolled the virtues of the traditional family. 'Children from these families,' he said, 'tend to do better physically, educationally and emotionally.'

'It is a sad fact,' Mr Fabricant concluded, 'that more than a third of all families in our society are single parent families. There are many apologists for that – many people who try to justify it or even defend it. I believe that there can be no substitute for the traditional family.'[1]

Mr Fabricant's defence of the 'traditional family' idyll is both genial and heartwarming, and its message permeates the Children Act in subtle and far-reaching ways.

The Act rests on the belief that children are generally best cared for within the family, with both parents playing a full part and without resort to legal proceedings. It introduces too the concept of parental responsibility to sum up the collection of duties, rights and authority that parents have in respect of their children. Within that general context, it emphasises, first and foremost, the paramountcy of the child's welfare.

ADVICE

The advice to the local authorities quoted in *The Care of Children: Principles and Practice in Regulations and Guidance*[2] states firmly that since there are unique advantages for children in experiencing normal family life in their own birth family, every effort should be made to preserve the child's home and family links. This, it is stated, can best be achieved by the development of a working partnership with parents who should 'be expected and enabled to retain their responsibilities and to remain as closely involved as is consistent with their child's welfare, even if that child cannot live at home either temporarily or permanently'. Family links should also be maintained. Great care should be taken to avoid unwanted intrusion into family life and throughout the Act we hear about the duties and responsibilities of 'reasonable parents'.

May I venture to suggest that, although it may not be immediately apparent to Mr Fabricant, not many of the children who are subject to child abuse investigations are very happy. Nor are they doing well physically, educationally and emotionally. Sadly, although Mr Fabricant clearly does not like it, few of these children come from what could be described as a traditional family, i.e. one man legally married to one woman with however many progeny. Tragic though it may be and for whatever reason, parents in these children's lives have fallen somewhat short of what Mr Fabricant might consider should be their aim, i.e. 'to promote the good health, well-being and happiness of children'.

Over the years our organisation, SACCS/Leaps and Bounds, has worked directly with many hundreds of abused children who have required the protection of the courts. Mention traditional family life and few of these children would have much idea of the concept, let alone whether or not they had experienced it. For many of these small people their experience of 'family life' has often been a confused and precarious *mélange* peppered with 'here today, gone tomorrow' figures. Coupled with this, many have suffered an ongoing catalogue of abuse, humiliation, degradation and sexual torture at the hands and genitalia of care givers of a nature beyond the scope of the imagination of many of us more fortunate human beings. For many of us, family life has engendered the comforting and reassuring belief that children, being small and vulnerable, have the right to receive love, security, care and protection.

Implicit in the Children Act is the assumption that most if not all parents are inherently reasonable, and furthermore that, as reasonable parents, they will understand the physical, emotional and educational needs of their children. Also implicit in the Act lies the expectation that parents will possess both the commitment and wherewithal to meet their children's needs; and tacit in this thinking is the premise that, even for those parents who do not come up to the mark, with enough participation and cooperation with 'caring professionals' a tolerable quality of life for their children can be achieved within the child's family context. Failing all of this, the assumption continues, parents will, with help and guidance, be in a position to maintain 'family links' and contribute positively to the child's welfare.

Let us not doubt that for a proportion of children this logic may be supported by reality, for there surely exists a majority of children whose families are either wonderful, good, mediocre or bad, but not too bad, however they are composed and whatever the social and economic pressures upon them. There are many good things to be said about the Children Act. The increased flexibility which the Act provides in issuing different orders for different circumstances provides many more options for children. The emphasis on listening to children and eliciting wishes and feelings is surely a breakthrough. Stringent registration and inspection of children's establishments are examples of positive progress.

It is, however, the children who suffer most within our society who are arguably the very children who are most in need of the protection of the law. One of the most tragic weaknesses in the Act is that it apparently fails completely to take into account what we as a society already know about the characteristics of people, parents or otherwise, who abuse their children, in physical, emotional and sexual ways. For children, in particular those who are sexually abused, would appear to fare very badly under the new legislation.

SEXUAL ABUSE

Child sexual abuse is a significant reality: 'it is estimated that 8% of men and 12–16% of women in the UK have experienced sexual abuse as children'.[3] We know that the majority of child sexual abuse takes place within the family, not outside it.[4] We know too that physical, sexual and emotional abuse are linked and often occur in the same context. We know that, generally speaking, people who abuse children seldom do it publicly. We know that children are often threatened, coerced or bribed to keep such skeletons in the family cupboard. The professional literature burgeons with such information. We know that sexual abuse is a syndrome of secrecy and denial.[5]

In cases where child sexual abuse is a reality, Suzanne Sgroi,[6] for example, traces a predictable progression inherent in the dynamics of child sexual abuse when it occurs within a family. This begins with the disclosure phase where the information comes to light and the child and family are exposed. This is rapidly followed by the denial phase. Denial typically happens within the whole family system. Subsequently a suppression phase begins where the offender(s) works hard to ensure, using various strategies, that no further information comes to light. At this point the 'family' system typically closes ranks in secrecy. Usually this culminates in retraction when the fearful child is unable to sustain a position and cannot remember or does not know. As a practitioner I have watched this process happening on countless occasions.

THE GROWN-UPS

What of the grown-ups who perpetrate these acts? Literature and research in sex-offending behaviour tells us that sex offenders seldom take responsibility for their behaviour. The field is in its relative infancy in the treatment of adult sex offenders. We know, however, that sex offenders do not suddenly stop offending, because their behaviour is apparently driven by a complex and deep emotional need to obtain sexual gratification from children's bodies.

Information on Post Traumatic Stress[7] indicates that the human mind has a mechanism which can sustain survival at times of overwhelming psychological stress. Children commonly use dissociation to defend against unbearable psychological pain. Rape and abuse by care givers are unbearably psychologically painful. These psychological defence mechanisms play havoc with the accurate recall required in the courtroom process. The experience of abuse often has devastating and far-reaching effects on physical, emotional and mental health long into the future.[8] In these children's lives where this type of abuse features, family values must surely represent, at best, a weak and ineffectual bastion of defence.

The Cleveland Inquiry did not hear evidence on what current available research could offer on patterns in family violence or sex-offending behaviour. The judge was given a narrow brief and such considerations were apparently not pertinent to it. Had such information been taken into account, then arguably legislators like Mr Fabricant might have been better informed.

PROJECT

Our Leaps and Bounds Project currently consists of three small houses in the community, all registered under the Children Act as children's homes. Each house is home to five small children, all under 8 years old on admission. All of our children have a history of gross physical, emotional and sexual abuse. Frequently they have been previously rehabilitated home to suffer more abuse. Because of their level of need, which cannot be met by resources within their own local authorities, they are placed with us by authorities from all over the country. Leaps and Bounds is a specialist resource. In a sense the children referred to it are at the end of the line, for the legacy of their abuse has rendered them unable to live comfortably alongside other people. Often predominant among a myriad of complex difficulties is their out-of-control sexual behaviour. These are children who can neither live within their families of origin, nor can they be currently contained in alternative families.

Slowly and painstakingly, our staff begin the task of containing the behaviour of these children in a loving holding environment, integrating them into mainstream school and offering intensive therapeutic work in the play room. In short, it is a structural underpinning job. Eventually, a process of recruiting and training permanent or individual carers can begin. After placement these children may need continued help on an ongoing basis. These are resilient and resourceful little people. Some are lucky to have escaped with their lives.

Little by little the full extent of the pain and distress which has characterised their short lives reveals itself as they begin to make sense of the chaotic existence they have lived. Details of their abuse which accompanies their arrival on the project is typically a small proportion of the extent of the abuse which eventually reveals itself in therapy. The odds are already firmly stacked against these children. Their adjustment to a more conventional reality will clearly be fraught with difficulty. Often they have been robbed of the opportunity to fulfil their potential as human beings.

What impact, then, was the Children Act likely to have on the lives of these, the most vulnerable of our children? All of the fifteen children in our care are currently subject to care orders. A significant proportion of these were made prior to the implementation of the Children Act. But of those children more recently before the court for the first time, what general trends can we discern? Let us look at some of the circumstances in more detail.

DARRYL

Darryl was 6 and his sister Kelly Marie was 4 when care orders were made some months ago. He was a premature baby, the survivor of twins, who consistently failed to thrive. At the age of 2 he went to nursery where he voraciously ate other children's leftovers, often off the floor. He masturbated until he was sore and attempted to grab other children's genitals. He was not a regular attender. His father, legally married to his mother, resented, it seemed, any intrusion into his family life. Darryl did not have a social worker for a long time despite the pleas of the nursery staff. For eight months his file sat, like many other similar ones, in a pile marked 'unallocated'.

When he did arrive at nursery, Darryl often had bruising on the tops of his arms, the back of his ears and around the upper legs and buttocks. His bottom was often sore and red. He smelt. Eventually, when Darryl was 3 years and 9 months old, action was taken. The first of a number of child abuse investigations took place, revealing copious suspicious injuries, bruises, lacerations and bizarre burns to the feet – all inconclusive.

A visit to Darryl's bedroom revealed an unheated room, stinking mattress, no floor covering and one sodden blanket. It also revealed a rope used to tie the child to the bed. Darryl himself, it seems, was not formally interviewed for the simple reason that he did not talk much sense. His behaviour was bizarre. When he was not talking to the fish in the nursery fish tank, or the garden swing, he was running around frantically in an agitated state, shouting foul language at people, or recoiling in fear when anyone unfamiliar approached.

In the meantime sterling efforts were taking place to work with his parents. His father was often drunk, his mother unable to assert herself. Contracts were drawn up based on the assumption that Darryl's parents needed help to recognise that their children had needs and that they could be helped to meet these needs. They did not and they could not. The nursery reported that Darryl's mother lacked motivation when they tried to teach her how to feed and bathe her children. Material help was poured into the family. The social worker's contracts became more detailed: 'At 7.30 you need to set the alarm to get up. Get Darryl up first and bathe and wash him in warm water and dress him in clean clothes. Put some Cornflakes in a plate and pour some milk on with a spoon of sugar.'

Eventually, after many months, attempts to enhance the quality of Darryl's existence and encourage parental responsibility palpably failed. There was another child abuse investigation – this time application for an interim order was made.

By the time he came to the project, Darryl had been through two foster homes and a failed rehabilitation attempt to his mother in the space of six months. She finally left her husband after a violent argument. Now a social worker brings her to see him. He approaches her with caution – she smiles and says 'hello'. Darryl then goes off to divert himself elsewhere in the room, looking up occasionally and guardedly when she attempts to talk to him. For the most part he is busily oblivious. Neither initiates any physical contact. He talks incessantly about Kelly Marie and is overjoyed to see her.

Play Sessions

In his play sessions we hear bit by bit about the monster who wee-weed on his tummy and in his mouth, the soap and the wee-wee he was forced to swallow and the electric curling tongs apparently used on his penis.

At night the bedtime ritual begins when he surrounds himself 'in my clean nice bed' with 'Action Men' and cuddly toys to guard him. Clutching his duvet tightly, 'been a good boy today' he asks searchingly. Half statement, half question. Always the same answer: 'Darryl's wonderful. Darryl's a hero. He is.' He settles down to sleep in the knowledge that his blanket will not be taken away because he has been naughty, in order that he can endure the discomfort of being cold all night (one of the monster's more subtle persecutory strategies, it appears).

Local Authority

The local authority concerned worked very hard in Darryl's case to preserve the integrity of his family life. Somewhere the paramountcy principle got lost in the morass of Mr Fabricant's family values. The 'unique
advantages' to Darryl of life within his family are not immediately
apparent. In fact, Darryl was lucky that his case came to the top of the
pile. Darryl had the additional misfortune of living in an area where provision is already stretched to the limit, and the social workers also have
to face the 'presumption of no order' introduced by the Children Act.
Once need has been established and steps taken to protect him, what
provision can be made for the particular needs of this child? The battle
for resources for Darryl has begun. Cases such as Darryl's pose additional problems for local authorities – there is often not enough money
to fulfil their obligations under the Act. There are often worries that the
case may go to Appeal. The more impecunious local authorities cannot
afford to have costs awarded against them.

Meanwhile back in the House, according to Mr Fabricant the government have 'recognised the duty of care and are fulfilling their obligation'.
The Act, we hear, has been 'widely hailed as a great success'. Earlier in
the debate his Honourable friend Mr Bowis, the Parliamentary Under-
Secretary of State for Health, has reassured the House that since the
implementation of the Act, events have shown a marked decrease in the
number of emergency protection orders:

> following the implementation of the Children Act 2,215 children were subject
> to Emergency Protection Orders, giving authority for the child to be removed
> from home. That compares with 4,677 children removed to a place of safety the
> previous year under the Children and Young Persons Act 1969. These are clear
> indications of how new practices and social workers working in co-operation
> with parents, as the Act intended, can make the system work better.

Darryl was a number in that statistical shortfall. His voice was not heard
and he does not have a vote.

Where does Darryl go from here? The 'preservation of the family links'
argument will doubtless loom large in vital decisions regarding future
contact with his mother (there is no extended family). Erudite closing

speeches will doubtless wax lyrical about the duty to promote and sustain links with his mother. It says so in the Children Act. Now established, Darryl's mother's once-fortnightly contact could continue, couldn't it? After all, he does not have any other family links in his life. At least for the time being, his behavioural difficulties currently preclude the option of an alternative family. Darryl is still learning the difference between loving and hurting. Some of the violence he acts out could seriously damage other people. At the moment he needs more specialised care than an ordinary family could offer.

LEANNE

Two years ago 7-year-old Leanne was in Darryl's shoes. Leanne is of mixed parentage; her father is of Asian extraction. A victim of sexual abuse in her large extended family group, Leanne has not had contact with them for a number of years. She had lived in three foster homes before she and her brother were placed for adoption with her two younger sisters. They were subsequently adopted last year, in a family who somehow could not take to her and eventually wanted her to leave. During her first week with us Leanne would position herself under the dining room table and scream again and again. At the Christmas party she sat on Santa's knee and asked him if he would make babies with her. She often made that request of men. Leanne wanted to be a nice girl and she knew how to please grown-ups. She learned that long ago. Another, hitherto insurmountable, problem for her was that her adoptive parents did not like it. Nor did they like it when their 14-year-old boy was consistently propositioned. Nobody talked about it, though – it was all a bit embarrassing. Over the last two years we have talked about it as often as Leanne needs to – which is frequently. She is learning to like and respect her broken body. Leanne has learned that little girls do not have to offer sex for love. Leanne laughs a lot now. She has blossomed at school. She loves life and has learned to be assertive. She wants a new mummy and daddy, or at least a mummy, just for her – 'soon please'.

A guardian ad litem came to see Leanne the other day. Her first question was 'Have you got a new mummy and daddy for me?' No such luck – the guardian had a different brief. In a court halfway across the country, leave had been given to a sister of Leanne's natural mother to make application for a contact order. Leanne wrinkles her nose and trawls her memory. She thinks she can remember which auntie this is. Does she want to see her? She's not bothered. As grown-ups in loco parentis, however, we are, because court time in her area is at a premium and it will probably be another six months before this case is resolved – six more incomprehensible, frustrating and possibly irrelevant months for Leanne to wait.

ROBBIE

Blue-eyed, blond-haired cherubic little Robbie was born with mild spina bifida. Robbie's thoughts centre on sexual violence and his dad. Robbie is a predator. He needs constant supervision because he has not learned to take care of his body yet, and we have to help him to learn. He masturbates to fantasies of rape and creates opportunities to coerce other children into sex acts with him against their will – like his dad. His dad is in prison for violent criminal offences. Robbie saw the blood. Robbie has been in care seventeen times. His adoptive placement also failed. His night terrors wake the neighbours. He thinks his dad is coming to get him – and he really is.

Robbie's dad is out of prison, and has recently been informed of his legal rights. Since in this case the care order was granted before the Act came into force, he now wishes to make application for a residence order. He has hired an enquiry agent to locate Robbie's crack-addicted mother. Soon further assaults are likely to take place – this time on the legal aid fund. Robbie does not know about all of this yet. It is a new development. He has only just started a new school – soon both the school and our staff group will be living with the impact of all this. We have a long way to go with Robbie.

Robbie was never going to be easy to place in a family. Traditional families do not exactly queue up to offer permanent homes for children like him. Robbie's pathology and the ways in which it is acted out in his behaviour are an offence to family values and if – no, not if, *when* – we are able to find a home for him and a suitable and probably remarkable family wish to adopt him, we will no doubt be considering at some length the question of adoption with contact. Then the remarkability of that remarkableness will be put to the test when the family are asked to welcome not only Robbie but also his parents into their lives. Because if Robbie was asked tomorrow if he wanted to see his dad, he would say 'yes'. What Robbie's dad wants is what Robbie wants – no question. And no amount of *Memorandum of Good Practice* interviews will induce Robbie to tell on his dad.

Children like Leanne and Darryl and Robbie do not fare terribly well under interviewing protocol such as the *Memorandum*. They often cannot remember, or they do not want to remember, or they do not know. Sometimes it is too dangerous to know. It is hardly surprising, then, that few abusers are brought to justice. At the same time, of course, there are the rather ludicrous new duties upon local authorities to seek cooperation and permission from parents to interview the child in the investigation of allegations of possible offences against children like Robbie. Common sense might dictate that issues of such complexity demand a slow and cautious approach. Such an approach is very difficult under the Act which demands that once the information comes to light, evidence ought to be collected within weeks – the time scale of EPOs, assessment orders and interim orders. There is no doubt that the 1993/4 Government statistics will outline a further welcome reduction in the number of cases of child sexual abuse coming before criminal courts and a concomitant reduction in the number of applications in civil courts under the Children Act.

Come, come, gentlemen! Adjust the rose-tinted spectacles! What is being protected here? Vulnerable children or family values? Herein lies a fundamental dilemma: these do not and cannot go hand in hand. When you do your deciding – at the 'Deciding Place', the biggest and most important 'Deciding Chamber' in the land – please can you be sensible and grown up, listen very carefully (even to things that are not nice to hear about the things other grown-ups do), switch off your own (political) agendas and make a law that really protects our abused children.

REFERENCES

1. House of Commons Official Report, Parliamentary Debates, vol. 227, no. 203 (Hansard), (London, HMSO, 25 June 1993).
2. *The Care of Children: Principles and Practice in Regulation and Guidance* (London, HMSO, 1989).
3. Baker and Duncan, 'Child Sexual Abuse: A Study of Prevalence in Britain', *Child Abuse and Neglect*, 8: 4, (1985), pp. 457–67.
4. Suzanne Sgroi, *Handbook of Clinical Intervention in Child Sexual Abuse* (Lexington Books, 1989).
5. Tilman Furniss, *The Multi Professional Handbook of Child Sexual Abuse* (1991).
6. *Op. cit.* (n. 4).
7. Lenore Terr, *Too Scared to Cry* (New York, Harper & Row, 1990).
8. Wyatt and Powell, *The Lasting Effects of Child Sexual Abuse* (Sage, 1988).

See also: *An Introduction to the Children Act* (London, HMSO, 1989).

Madge Bray, *Sexual Abuse: The Child's Voice/Poppies on the Rubbish Heap* (Canongate, 1990).

Martin Herbert, *Working with Children under the Children Act* (BPS Books, 1993).

Memorandum of Good Practice on Video Interviews with Child Witnesses for Criminal Proceedings (London, HMSO, 1992).

Steven Wolf, 'What Sex Offenders Tell us about Prevention Strategies', *Child Abuse and Neglect*, 13 (1989), pp. 293–301.

5

The Criminal Process and the Child Witness in Sexual Abuse Cases

Michael Lawson QC

The Cleveland Inquiry and the Children Act have between them wrought a sea-change in both the attitudes and the practices of the courts and those involved in them in relation to child abuse in its various forms. The criminal courts now remain the only places where children still regularly attend to give evidence and are still cross-examined about sexual activities which many adults have difficulty in discussing publicly.

Is this a relic of a system which has traditionally relied heavily on oral evidence, a perverse desire by criminal practitioners to practise their skills on 'easy' targets or an inevitable and unhappy consequence of the criminal process? A moment's reflection on the purpose of a criminal trial provides the answer. Such hearings are in sharp contrast to proceedings under the Children Act 1989 where the child's welfare is the court's paramount consideration. Once the decision to prosecute has been taken, the focus of the criminal trial is the proof of the defendant's guilt. In the majority of cases of child sexual abuse (CSA) it is likely that the child will provide the only evidence of the guilt of the person charged. Medical evidence, if there is any, is often not conclusive either of the fact of abuse or of the perpetrator of it, and may be of slight value where proof 'beyond reasonable doubt' is the standard required. Concern for the 'child's welfare' becomes in this type of trial little more than the immediate duty of the court to ensure that those who give evidence are subjected to the least possible trauma and distress. Is that sufficient in a system which, following the 1989 Act, is intended to apply 'common principles of law to all proceedings concerning children whether in the public or private law field'?[1] Nothing in that legislation resolves the dilemma of the conflict between the public interest in the detection of crime and conviction of the guilty on the one hand, and on the other, the welfare of the child who has to shoulder the burden of the prosecution, in many cases, of a member or close friend of the family. That task carries with it the knowledge that the exercise will either sound the death knell for the family which has provided the only security the child has known, or lead to recriminations and bitterness. All that, before one considers the trauma of the trial itself, suggests that the question of whether there should be a trial at all is one that merits very anxious consideration.

WHETHER TO PROSECUTE

This is not a question in which the civil courts have been anxious to become involved, nor a decision that the police traditionally have wished to share. Booth J set out the position in unequivocal terms in delivering judgment[2] on an application by police for disclosure of records and video recordings made by wards, then in the care of the local authority, so that a police investigation of allegations of sexual abuse could progress:

> The protection afforded to a child by the exercise of the wardship jurisdiction should not be extended to the point where it gives protection to offenders against the law. The court must take into consideration as a matter of public policy, the need to safeguard not only its wards but other children against the harm they may suffer as the result of recurring crimes by undetected criminals. The likely outcome and its effects on a ward of granting an application such as the police now make must be considered in each and every case. But when balanced against the competing public interest which requires the court to protect society from the perpetration of crime it could only be *in exceptional circumstances* that the interests of the individual ward should prevail.

While the application was made so that an investigation could take place, the judge specifically referred to the consequence of the ruling, namely that 'it could lead to the direct involvement of the ward in criminal proceedings ... a fact which could be regarded as detrimental to his or her interests'. There is no reason to suppose that the position has materially changed since 1987.

The position of the police has been equally clearly stated: 'In this context as in all others, the prosecution of offences is a matter which rests by law within the discretion of the chief officer of police concerned ...'[3] Where a case conference has been held, he is enjoined to 'take into account any views expressed ... about the effect of an investigation on the welfare of the child' whilst retaining the right to take contrary action. The Code of Practice issued in 1987 by the Metropolitan Police echoed that principle.[4] No doubt as the police child protection units work increasingly closely with other agencies, decisions to charge will be taken 'in committee', although it is difficult to imagine that their opinion would be lightly disregarded.

In many cases, of course, there is insufficient evidence to lay charges – either because no abuse has taken place, or because the child is unable or unwilling for obvious reasons to 'disclose'. Where, however, an investigation provides some apparently reliable evidence – for example, the video interview of the child – a charge will often follow. It is obviously easy to criticise decisions to prosecute with the benefit of hindsight and without access to the background information available to those who make the decision. Some cases coming to the Crown Court, however, strongly suggest that where there is considered to be sufficient evidence, the perceived public interest in prosecuting outweighs the interests of the child.

REALISTIC PROSPECT

Where the decision to charge is made, the Crown Prosecution Service (CPS) is then bound to consider whether there is a realistic prospect of conviction. Practitioners know only too well that it is an impossibly difficult task in this type of case where the taking of the history of events must be deliberately uncritical. The abolition of live evidence at committal or on transfer means that the first occasion that the evidence can be judged is at the trial itself. The number of cases that result in acquittal is proof, if it were needed, of our current inability to estimate reliably the prospects of conviction in CSA cases on the basis of the trial papers alone. To provide an effective review of the prospects of conviction, the CPS must surely be given greater access to the background material then available. The decision to prosecute has devastating consequences for witnesses and defendants. Those that have to make it must be given the best possible chance of getting it right.

THE TRIAL PROCESS

The trial process in cases of CSA, whether a trial at the magistrates' court or trial by jury following committal proceedings, has to balance the undoubted public interests in the conviction of the guilty and the protection of the innocent with the public concern about the trauma and damage that the criminal justice system can inflict on the child required to give evidence. Substantial changes both in practice and in the procedural and evidential law have occurred since 1988. These are designed to improve the prosecution of alleged offenders in this type of case without damaging essential safeguards against wrongful conviction, while at the same time reducing the stress and distress involved where a child provides the crucial evidence upon which the prosecution has been brought.

Those involved in criminal trials have been acutely aware of the enormous demands made of the child witness but conscious too that it is in such emotionally charged cases that a defendant requires the greatest protection against wrongful conviction. Changes to assist the child to give evidence more effectively must not be made at the expense of those safeguards that protect a defendant's legitimate rights. The recent changes have concentrated on making it less traumatic for the child to give evidence.

Outside court better facilities have been provided for interviewing and for medical examinations; police and social workers have received specialist training in interviewing techniques; there is a greater recognition of the need for continuity of contact with the child, although as in many areas, financial and manpower restraints render practice less satisfactory than it might be. In particular there is a need for a more consistent approach to the provision of someone to be with the child while at court and while giving evidence. More often than not, some new and unknown person is provided just before trial for this purpose. It should not be difficult to institute a system whereby an adult unconnected with the case (perhaps provided by a voluntary agency such as Victim Support) who has experience of the court system and of children, can be introduced to the child sufficiently in advance of trial for the child to feel able to talk freely about all matters relating to trial, before, during and after the event. Apart from this aspect, there is generally a greater awareness of the needs of witnesses – improved facilities at many, but not all, courts and prior visits to the courtroom to see what a court looks like reduce the fear that many experience. The recently produced 'Child Witness Pack' published by the NSPCC but developed by an impressive array of government and voluntary agencies is designed to explain to children and their parents how the legal system works and their role in it and is to be welcomed as a further example of the help being given to young witnesses.

LEGISLATIVE CHANGE

The principal reforms have been introduced by the Criminal Justice Acts of 1988 and 1991. Prior to the earlier Act, trials involving child witnesses had largely followed the procedures used for all criminal trials. Courts had, however, already permitted the use of screens to shield children giving evidence from the dock and at the Old Bailey I introduced a specially designed screened witness box, equipped with microphone and placed out of view of the public gallery so that only the judge, jury and counsel could see or be seen by the witness. A video camera in front of the witness box provided a television picture to the defendant of the child giving evidence. Properly designed and located, such a screened witness box provides an ideal combination of security from the defendant with the encouragement that the prosecuting advocate can provide through face-to-face contact.

Changes introduced by the two Acts have sought to introduce improvements in three main areas: the committal proceedings; the procedural rules relating to the corroboration of children's evidence; and the manner in which evidence is given.

COMMITTAL PROCEEDINGS

Most allegations of CSA are tried at the Crown Court by judge and jury. In consequence committal proceedings had to take place and children were often required to give evidence and be cross-examined both there and at the trial itself. This was usually at the defence insistence, although in some cases the Crown was anxious to check whether the evidence would be sufficiently strong to justify the full trial.

Section 32 of the Criminal Justice Act 1988 precluded the calling of a child as a witness by the Crown in cases involving sexual offences, child cruelty, assault or injury or threats of injury. Written records of the child's account became admissible in place of oral testimony. If the legislators thought that such a provision would make much difference to the number of children required to give evidence twice, they were mistaken. Defence advocates, knowing that the live television link provisions (see below) would apply at the Crown Court, vigorously exercised their right to confront children at the magistrates' court. That has now been corrected by s. 55(1) of the Criminal Justice Act 1991 which prevents children in cases involving the same class of offences, and young people in relation only to offences of a sexual nature, from giving evidence at the magistrates' court except where the trial is to take place at that court. Much more fundamental, however, is the extension of the 'transfer' provisions first introduced for complex fraud trials to these s. 32 cases.

By s. 53 of the Criminal Justice Act 1991 the Director of Public Prosecutions may serve a 'Notice of Transfer' on the magistrates' court where the Director is of the opinion that there is sufficient evidence for committal; that a child who is either the victim of, or has witnessed the commission of, an offence will be called to give evidence at trial; and that 'for the purpose of avoiding any prejudice to the welfare of the child' the case should be proceeded with without delay by the Crown Court. The last condition will almost certainly reduce delay and improve the quality of the child's recollection. Possibly more importantly, if the cases are heard speedily, it will allow the child to begin the process of recovery from the abuse and, where necessary, receive therapy. Until the child's evidence has been given, it is dangerous to the integrity of the evidence and unfair on the child as a witness to allow therapy to take place.

There is a further protection against witnesses having to give evidence twice contained in Schedule 6, para. 5(5) of the 1991 Act, which prohibits the trial judge from hearing evidence from child witnesses where there is an application by the defence for dismissal of the charges after transfer. Current practice suggests that the CPS will avail themselves, wherever possible, of these provisions. The abolition of committal proceedings altogether, now recommended by the Royal Commission[5] (Recommendation No. 116) should cater for those other cases where young witnesses fall outside the unnecessarily complicated age provisions contained in the latest Act.

COMPETENCE AND CORROBORATION

It is beyond the scope of this chapter, and probably beyond the ability of most practitioners and commentators, to provide a full and yet comprehensible account of the law on these two subjects and their interaction. Before 1988 children could give evidence on oath, if they understood the nature of the oath. If they did not, evidence would be given unsworn, provided that the child was of sufficient intelligence to give evidence and understand the duty of speaking the truth. This distinction compelled the judge to ask the witness a series of superficial questions, in order to determine whether the evidence should be on oath or not. Given that many adults would have difficulty, in this secular age, in distinguishing between telling the truth and telling the truth on oath, the exercise had little usefulness. For the child witnesses the questions must have come as an unnecessary and perhaps even offensive distraction at the beginning of their time in the witness box. The importance of the distinction lay in the directions that needed to be given to a jury. Evidence of children needed to be corroborated because they were children, and unsworn evidence of one child could not be corroborated by the unsworn evidence of another unsworn child. Both those rules of law were repealed by s. 34 of the Criminal Justice Act 1988, while the two categories of evidence and the questioning remained. Section 52 of the Criminal Justice Act 1991 has been passed to deal with that irritation by simply enacting that a witness under 14 years will give evidence unsworn. Witnesses over that age will give sworn evidence. Their competence to give evidence will be determined by the court in the same way as it would be in the case of any other adult witness. There has been academic criticism of the wording of this latter part of the section on the grounds that, on one interpretation, the test of competence for children requires a higher level of understanding than before.[6] It must be hoped that trial judges will interpret the Act according to the spirit and not the wording of the section!

Corroboration is still required in complaints of a sexual nature. Its technicalities remain a problem for judges, practitioners and juries alike and provide an endless source of appeals to the Court of Appeal. Will the legislators take any more notice of the Royal Commission Recommendation No. 195[7] than they have of either the Pigot Committee or the Law Commission and abolish the rule entirely?

GIVING EVIDENCE

The use of screens was a practical move by the courts to make the giving of evidence less stressful. Legislative change was required for any further developments in this direction. The first step was taken by s. 32 of the Criminal Justice Act 1988, which for the first time permitted live evidence to be given from outside the actual courtroom by means of a television link, provided that the child was under the age of 14, that the trial was on indictment and that the offence was one of those listed in that section. Those restrictions meant that children still had to give evidence in court in all proceedings at the magistrates' court, and that witnesses aged over 14 were not able to benefit (a limit now raised to 17 in sexual cases by s. 54(7) of the 1991 Act).

This section does far more than merely tinker with age limits, for it contains within it the most radical provisions relating to the evidence of young people in these sensitive cases. It is based on the recommendations of the Home Office Advisory Group on Video Evidence which reported at the end of 1989 (the Pigot Report). As happens so often, the recommendations were implemented only in part. As always, it is the intended beneficiaries of the change who will suffer. To suggest that failure to implement the new procedure in its entirety was cost related is possibly to be too cynical, because there are some respectable arguments against it. None was incapable of resolution, however, and the majority of those who would have been most affected were prepared to countenance the substantial changes in work patterns and priorities necessary to ensure that no child would have to give evidence in court at the trial unless it was by choice.

Video Recording

The section permits a video recording of an interview with a child in all s. 32 cases, or a young person where it is a sexual offence, to be given in evidence with the leave of the court. Leave will not be granted where the witness will not be available for cross-examination or where the court is of the opinion that in the interests of justice the recording, or parts of it, should not be admitted. Where leave is given the recording replaces the evidence-in-chief. The witness is then cross-examined by the defence advocate, s. 55(7) of the Criminal Justice Act 1991 having removed the right of an accused to conduct cross-examination of such witnesses in person.

Major problems arise from this sequence. The first is that the witness is subjected to examination from the defence without any preliminary questions from the Crown to assist the witness to 'tell the story'. The prosecution is specifically precluded from asking questions by subs. 5 which states:

> Where a video recording is admitted under this section –
> a) the child witness shall be called by the party who tendered it in evidence;
> b) that witness *shall not be examined in chief* on any matter which, in the opinion of the court, has been dealt with in his recorded testimony.

The prosecution advocate will be hamstrung by the format of the interview and the child will be unnecessarily at the mercy of the defence. Take the case of the child who, in the early interview, is too embarrassed to give the full details of a particular event, or who for similar reasons gives an account that is hopelessly out of chronological sequence. Under these procedures the prosecution is unable to assist the witness to give a full and ordered account and the defence are able to comment adversely on what may appear as elaborations of the original account. There can be few interviews in this type of case where, however skilled the interviewer, the recording adequately represents the full detail of the account the child can give or the effect of events upon the child. Moreover it is likely that the prosecution advocate, with the advantage of an overall view of all the evidence, will wish to place greater emphasis on some parts of the case than on others, to deal with apparent inconsistencies and clear up ambiguous aspects of the account. None of this is, at present, possible. The purposes of, and the techniques required by, those conducting interviews are quite different from those of the advocate who needs to present a clear and compelling account to the tribunal, whether judge or jury. Can the calling of a child witness be justified where the limitations imposed by the trial process put the witness at an unfair disadvantage? Many prosecuting advocates will take the view that, while this restriction exists, it will be better to call the child to give evidence either in court or through the live television link than to labour under the disadvantages inherent in this new provision.

Criticism

The overwhelming criticism of this procedure is, of course, that the witness still has to give evidence at trial and still has the stress of waiting until the court and the defence are ready to hear the case. Had the recommendation been implemented, both 'remedial' examination-in-chief and cross-examination would have taken place at one time under the auspices of the trial judge, well in advance of the trial, in some appropriate place, allowing child witnesses to put the events behind them and the defence to prepare their case with full knowledge of the evidence to be called. The whole of the witness's account would be recorded and would form the evidence at trial. Changes are already being made to parts of the 1991 Act. Let them not be the last.

IMPROVEMENT IN THE QUALITY OF JUSTICE?

The very welcome changes made in the last few years were designed to remove, and have to an extent succeeded in removing, unnecessary impediments to the effective prosecution of those who are guilty of CSA and to assist the child witnesses to give evidence to the best of their ability, at the least cost to their welfare.

The quality of justice, however, depends not solely on the fact that the evidence is given but also on its reliability and proper appreciation of its significance. The ability of the judges of fact to assess both these aspects is obviously vital. If that tribunal is a professional judge trained in Children Act work, with a lifetime's relevant experience and with the availability of expert assistance from various professional disciplines to help where necessary, there is every chance that the evidence will be properly evaluated and justice achieved.

The Jury

What help, however, do the poor jurors receive to calculate the effect of the sequence and structure of the interview on the weight to be placed on the answers that result? What allowance should they make for initial denials of abuse or lack of detail in the early stages of disclosure, and how should they regard evidence of apparently precocious or promiscuous behaviour? What assistance do they get to help with that fundamental question of whether the witness is intrinsically reliable – not unimportant when the effects of abuse on the young mind can be appallingly serious and the occurrence of damage is often all too readily apparent. The short answer, of course, is that they receive almost no help because the criminal courts have always been reluctant to turn jury trials into trials of conflicting expert opinion. Scientific information or opinion is permitted only where it is likely to be outside the experience and knowledge of the jury. Many judges would say that such matters were within the general experience and the common knowledge of ordinary people, particularly where to say otherwise might involve children in further interviews with child psychiatrists/psychologists instructed by the defence. But if judges in civil courts, determining similar issues, feel the need for such information in addition to full background reports, and if changes of behaviour over the period covered by the allegations assist the courts in determining whether abuse has occurred, should juries not be provided with the same material? To do otherwise is to turn the process into a very dangerous game of chance.

DISCOVERY AND PUBLIC INTEREST IMMUNITY

There is no formal procedure for discovery in criminal trials but no one involved in the legal system over the last few years can fail to be aware of the problems caused by the lack of full disclosure by the prosecution to the defence of material that has come into their possession in the course of the investigation but upon which they do not seek to rely at trial. The cases of Maguire and Ward,[8] among others, have highlighted not only the haphazard system in operation but also the real importance that attaches to the fullest possible disclosure. In each case convictions had to be quashed because there was available material which could have had a significant impact on the trial had it been known to the defence. In R v. *Saunders*,[9] Henry J ruled that material 'that had some bearing on the offence(s) charged and the surrounding circumstances of the case' should be disclosed, adding significantly that it was for the defence and not the prosecution to assess its potential utility, save where issues of public interest immunity (PII) arose.

Where sensitive documents are not involved, the position of 'unused material' in the prosecution's possession is clear for the most part. It must be made available to the defence and schedules are now routinely prepared to alert the defence to the range of material held by the investigating team. What has not yet been resolved is the position where, for example, officers from a police child protection team are given copies of social services material in relation to a child or family under investigation, with or without undertakings as to confidentiality. Does the local authority lose its claim to immunity against disclosure because it has waived it in relation to the police, or are the police in a similar position to the psychiatrist preparing a report for the local authority that makes use of the case conference reports? In *Re S & W*,[10] it was held that privilege had not been waived since the psychiatrist was an adviser to, and had a confidential relationship with, the local authority. It is not easy to classify the police/local authority relationship in that way. If privilege persists, can immunity be claimed by the police or only by the authority?

INFORMATION

It is the position of information held by the local authority or other third party, however, that gives rise to much greater concern to those involved in criminal trials. Common sense and experience suggest that there will sometimes be material of considerable significance in third-party files. While no one denies that such files should not be subjected to indiscriminate attention, some procedure must be created by which the prosecution as well as the defence are able, well in advance of trial, to identify those matters to which Henry J referred in *R v. Saunders*.[11] If a child's evidence may have been contaminated by others making similar allegations against the same defendant or the child has made previous untrue allegations, or has been in contact with someone whose wretched existence has been dramatically improved by the attention she has received since making an unfounded complaint, then the sooner both prosecution and defence are aware of it, the better. It does the genuine victims no favours when false complaints are exposed as such in the full publicity of a trial.

WITNESS SUMMONS

The system that operates at present is invariably initiated by the defence issuing a witness summons under s. 2 of the Criminal Procedure (Attendance of Witnesses) Act 1965. That requires the director of the appropriate social services department to attend at court and produce 'any document or thing specified in the Summons'. The usual response is to claim public interest immunity and leave the judge to decide which parts of the file, if any, should be disclosed to the defence. Sometimes the prosecution are provided with copies of the same material. Often they are not. There are obvious weaknesses, quite apart from the absence of any universally agreed procedure which can be applied in a consistent way in all cases. First, Henry J in *Saunders*[12] recognised that the defence were in the best position to decide what was likely to be relevant. The summons requires the documents sought to be specified, and does not permit the identification of areas of relevance to the issues in the trial. It is often not possible for the defence to identify the specific event or influence on the child that triggered the complaint and to specify the document(s) or the class of documents in which that information might be found without having seen them; nor can the judge be expected to examine the file to identify the documents – that is not the function of a judge. Second, unless the prosecution carry out the same procedure, they may not become aware, until the child is cross-examined, of matters that might have affected the decision to prosecute, or to continue a prosecution.

The sheer volume of some social services files has led one judge at first instance[13] to give a restricted interpretation to the wording of s. 2. He ruled that the question of consideration of particular documents in regard to public interest immunity only falls to be determined when there is a 'lawful and effective use of the limited powers under the 1965 Act'. He set out the three criteria for a lawful and effective use of the Act as follows:

> it means to produce to the Court any documents or thing *admissible in evidence* in the proceedings in course; and it means to produce to the Court any document or thing specified in the summons, and I emphasise the word specified.

> In order to have effect, a summons issued under Section 2 of the 1965 Act *must specify the document or thing required to be produced with reasonable particularity*. It must either be a document or thing individually identified, or if indirectly and not individually identified, identified by reference to a class of documents or things by which criterion the recipient of the summons can know what is the obligation which the Court places on him.

> The summons is not, in my judgement, a proper and effective order *if it requires the recipient to make judgements, for example, of relevance or weight*; to make

judgements in regard to other documents which may or may not be in his possession in order to try to determine the extent of his obligation under the order of the Court.

He discharged a summons, which sought the disclosure of material

which tended to show that the child had made statements inconsistent with or different from the proposed evidence or had been untruthful or guilty of dishonesty or had made complaints of a sexual nature against any person other than those revealed in the statements already disclosed and served on the defence.

The ruling will no doubt be welcomed by both judges and social service departments as a means of reducing the material to be examined and, if upheld, demonstrates the very limited discretion available to the trial judge to order disclosure. If the overriding test is 'admissibility in evidence' (recent decisions in relation to this section seem to confirm this limitation) and not 'materiality' to the issues in the case, very few documents will be subject to scrutiny. Is it really in the interests of justice, of the children and of defendants that relevant material affecting these serious issues should become largely inaccessible to the parties to the trial? Does the public interest demand such a restrictive interpretation of the Act?

Nothing could better illustrate the distinction between the civil and criminal jurisdictions than the ruling of Hollings J in *Re A and others*[14] in a disputed wardship case instituted by the local authority. He said:

in disputed cases such as these, both in the interests of the children and of justice to the parties, discovery ought to be given of original material recording matters of fact in relation to the children, their parents or other relevant persons, other than social workers, especially, of course transcripts and records of matters of interest ...

He added that even social work and analogous records enjoyed no absolute immunity against discovery.

It is an affront to any concept of fairness that a father, faced with serious allegations against him, would have access to relevant information in the civil courts, while his counterpart in criminal proceedings might well have none. The facts of that case vividly demonstrate the dangers of injustice that can flow from lack of disclosure. The local authority had presented their case by way of affidavits and affirmations. These proved, when compared with the material available to the local authority, to be not only 'exaggerated and one-sided' but also to present a picture that was 'quite misleading'.

BALANCE

There is undoubtedly a vitally important balance to be struck between the need for confidentiality in the creation of files concerning children and the need for the parties to the criminal trial to know, where there is material to assist, whether the complaint is genuine and undistorted by outside influences. There is no justification for the use of differing standards in different courts. Authoritative guidance is required as to the proper approach. A comprehensive practice direction would be welcomed by practitioners.

There can be no denial now that the prosecution of allegations of CSA has involved substantial departures from a number of the principles and rules that have governed the prosecution of other crimes. This is justified partly by the nature of the offences themselves and partly by the age of the witnesses involved. The processes of investigation and trial are now substantially less traumatic than they were even a few years ago. Nevertheless they remain experiences capable of causing further damage, particularly the ordeal of cross-examination, which is often mentally confusing and emotionally destructive. In an adversarial system it may not be possible to avoid such a testing procedure. Indeed by s. 54 of the 1991 Act the admission in evidence of a pre-recorded interview is statutorily dependent on the witness being available to be cross-examined. The full implementation of the Pigot recommendation would go a long way towards reducing the strain of that part of the trial. Prior disclosure of the defence case, recommended by the Royal Commission,[15] will also help to reduce the fear of cross-examination by ambush.

While the present system of criminal trial, requiring proof beyond a reasonable doubt, relies so heavily on the complainant witness, there is little chance of avoiding either harm to the child or damage to the rights that protect innocent defendants. Some would argue that neither is an acceptable price to pay. Those children who are able to explain what has happened to them are then required to undergo further trauma in support of society's pursuit of the sex offender. In so conducting our affairs, we encourage the abuser to select those young, vulnerable and disturbed children who are least likely to be able to withstand the ordeal and who are most likely to make unimpressive witnesses. We do so without protecting them from that abuse. Through our insistence on the child giving evidence, we ensure that many abusers never have to answer for their crimes.

COMBINATION OF JURISDICTIONS

Have we not gone as far as we should in adapting the present adversarial system for one category of case? Now that we have recognised the particular difficulties to which these cases give rise and created different rules and procedures where children are involved, is it not time to accept that a wholly different approach is required, probably more inquisitorial in nature? Let specialist judges, sitting if need be with a limited number of assessors or jurors, combine the criminal and civil jurisdictions in one trial, deciding all matters relating to the child, the defendant and the family unit where appropriate. Let that court, once decisions of fact have been reached, resolve all issues of disposal, having firmly in mind the paramount importance of the welfare of the child. Only then will it be possible to say that common principles of law truly apply to all proceedings concerning children.

REFERENCES

1. Sir Stephen Brown, President of the Family Division, 'Reform and the Rise of Family Law', *Inner Temple Yearbook*, 1993.
2. *Re S* [1987] Fam 199.
3. Home Office Circular No. 179/1976, Appendix 3, paras. 16–18.
4. *The Metropolitan Police Force Response to Child Abuse within the Family: Principles and Code of Practice*, para. 1.5: see A. Levy (ed.), *Focus on Child Abuse* (London, Hawksmere, 1989), pp. 147–62.
5. Royal Commission on Criminal Justice, Cm 2263 (London, HMSO, 1993).
6. See, for example, J. R. Spencer (1990) 140 New Law Journal, p. 1750, and Archbold News (July 1993).
7. *Op. cit.* (n. 5).
8. *R* v. *Maguire*, 94 Cr App R 133, CA; and *R* v. *Ward*, 96 Cr App R 1, CA.
9. *R* v. *Saunders and others*, CCC Transcript T881630, 1990.
10. [1983] 4 FLR 290, CA.
11. *Op. cit.* (n. 9).
12. *Ibid.*
13. *Per* HH Judge Laughland QC, *R* v. *Milner*, CCC, July 1993.
14. [1991] 1 WLR 1026, at 1301H.
15. *Op. cit.* (n. 5).

6

Beyond Child Abuse: a Child's Right to Physical Integrity

Peter Newell
Co-ordinator of EPOCH

To suggest that Henry Kempe and colleagues 'discovered' child battering in the 1960s is as insulting to the children who have been suffering it for centuries as the suggestion that Livingstone discovered the Victoria Falls was to the Africans who had been living there for centuries. Yet the former 'fact' seems to occur in most child abuse textbooks, just as the latter did in African school textbooks in colonial days.

Adult awareness and acknowledgement of adult cruelty to children, and of its effects not just on children but on the development of human societies, have grown steadily, the concern accelerating with more recent 'discoveries' of the extent of sexual abuse and institutional abuse.

This awareness and acknowledgement, however, will not be complete until adults have dropped the double standards and hypocrisy that still characterise their attitudes to violence and children in almost all societies around the world, and extend fully to children the protection from all forms of violence that they expect for themselves.

Child abuse is a concept invented by adults, and a large and growing adult industry has developed around it, doubtless motivated by genuine concern for children's welfare. The definition of child abuse in both common usage and professional practice, however, is incomplete and now does a disservice to children. It condones an arbitrary and quite high level of violence to them, while giving adults a comforting feeling of benevolent protection. Those working to end social and legal acceptance of violence to women did not use definitions that left some forms of violence acceptable, and that is probably because in those campaigns, adults – mostly women – were advocating on behalf of adults, unaffected by cultural conditioning which influences attitudes to children.

Adults, in most human societies, are now fully protected by law against all non-consensual physical assaults, including sexual assaults. Not only the law, but prevailing social attitudes condemn violence directed at adults. That does not mean, of course, that adults do not suffer interpersonal violence, in this or other societies; women in particular still suffer a high level of violence in their homes and elsewhere. You have, however, to go back to the eighteenth century to find legal authority for a husband's right to beat his wife, and then 'not in violent or cruel manner'.[1]

For adults the right to physical integrity and to protection from all inter-personal violence is regarded as a fundamental human right. In very few societies so far, however, has this right been extended to children. In most, when it comes to children, the law draws a special protective circle not around the child, but around the punishing parent or other carer.

The most common form of violence experienced by children in almost every country of the world is physical punishment: in their homes, in other childcare settings, in schools and in the penal system. There are many forms of physical punishment: smacking, slapping, belting, beating, whipping, scratching, pulling hair; forcing children to stay in uncomfortable positions, to do press-ups or to hold heavy weights. They involve in every case a large person deliberately inflicting a degree of pain or discomfort on a smaller person, and thus invading their physical integrity.

REASONABLE CHASTISEMENT

In 1889, the first law against cruelty to children passed through Parliament in England (seventy years after a similar measure to protect animals). Laws on assault pre-dated the Act, but had not been applied effectively to protect children. As the Bill passed through Parliament, MPs and peers showed that their major concern was to make quite sure that in legislating to reduce cruelty, they did nothing to limit parents', teachers' and other carers' rights to be cruel in the name of punishment. One MP implied that the instigators of the Bill, the recently formed Society for the Prevention of Cruelty to Children, intended to use it to 'prevent corporal punishment'. But the Bill as drafted specifically con-firmed the right to use 'reasonable and moderate punishment'. This was too limiting. Under pressure the government agreed to drop the words 'reasonable and moderate', although it was emphasised that this would make no practical difference as under common law only 'reasonable and moderate' punishment was lawful. In the House of Lords, a government minister reassured peers: 'Your lordships will see that the Bill carefully reserves intact the power which rests in a parent or guardian to administer punishment to a child.'[2]

That provision has been re-enacted without challenge or debate in succeeding Acts covering cruelty, including the still current Children and Young Persons Act 1933 which reads 'Nothing in this section shall be construed as affecting the right of any parent, teacher or other person having the lawful control or charge of a child or young person to administer punishment to him'; there are equivalent provisions in Acts covering Scotland and Northern Ireland.[3] There are plenty of cases in common law, going back over two centuries, which confirm the right of 'reasonable chastisement'. It is the existence of this right that explains why the law on assault had been entirely ineffective in protecting children from most adult assaults, although as far back as 1819 one distinguished legal commentator emphasised that 'Everyman's person [is] sacred, and no other [has] a right to meddle with it in the slightest manner.'[4]

The leading case dates back to 1860. It was brought against a schoolmaster after a 13-year-old boy died as a result of being taken from his bed at night and beaten with a thick stick and a skipping rope for two and a half hours. Cockburn CJ held that the teacher was liable to a charge of manslaughter, and he was convicted. The judge declared: 'By the law of England, a parent ... may for the purpose of correcting what is evil in the child, inflict moderate and reasonable corporal punishment, always, however, with this condition, that it is moderate and reasonable.'[5]

It is with that judgment, rooted clearly in the Victorian era and a belief in original sin, that the law rests today. As part of the British colonial 'heritage' this concept of 'reasonable' chastisement has been built, with little or no change, into the prevailing law in much of Africa, India, the United States and Canada, Australia and New Zealand, the Caribbean, etc. The rather patchy research that there has been into the origins of adult cruelty to children suggests that it has tended to follow enslavement, colonisation, military occupation and certain religious teaching. There is some evidence that in small-scale societies not subject to such influences, notably hunter-gatherer societies, the use of inter-personal violence or pain in child-rearing is unusual. Few such societies remain.

Have we really not moved beyond the Victorian benchmark of 'reason-ableness' in beating children? Hardly, it seems, and certainly not consis-tently. During the 1990s courts have considered a succession of cases in which parents had used implements to beat their children. The fact that the police and prosecuting authorities decided to proceed shows some change of attitudes. The overall direction of the judgments, however, has been scarcely reassuring to children. Scotland's most senior judge com-mented in a case in which a 9-year-old girl was bruised by a belting from her mother: 'It is evident that [the child] richly deserved punishment and that the mother's intention was to inflict upon her the punishment she deserved.'[6] At Brighton Crown Court in October 1991, a mother who had beaten her 11-year-old daughter with a garden cane and an electric flex was cleared of assault and cruelty. In March 1993, North Avon magistrates acquitted a father who admitted using a belt on his 5- and 8-year-old sons (although a clinical medical officer testified that she had only seen such injuries twice in ten years). In April 1993 at Southampton Crown Court, a mother was cleared of assault on appeal (she had slip-pered her 8-year-old daughter, causing heavy bruising). Judge McLean commented: 'In the words of one of my colleagues, if a parent cannot slipper a child, the world is going potty.'[7]

So, what does all this mean for the definition of child abuse? Even many professionals directly involved in child protection like to keep the concept in a different box to that of punishment, although they are daily confronted with the evidence that there is no distinction, that physical child abuse *is* punishment, which the perpetrator may or may not admit went 'a bit too far' (and much sexual abuse is also accompanied by pun-ishment). The only reason that they like to keep 'abuse' and 'punish-ment' in separate boxes is the highly personal nature of the issue. Whether you yourself were smacked or beaten as a child, or whether you have smacked your own young children, all of us have experienced childhood and adulthood in a society in which deliberately hurting and humiliating children is both legally and socially acceptable. We see it in the streets, in bus queues and in supermarkets on Saturday mornings. We do not like to think badly of our parents, or of ourselves, so we find it easier to operate double standards when forced to consider violence and children.

Changing the Culture

There is no doubt that the culture is changing, but not consistently. There has been accelerating progress to protect children from physical punishment (and in some cases from other humiliating forms of punishment too) outside the family home. One can see this as a logical progression from the reforms that led the state to drop the habit of physical punishment of adults: we stopped birching as a judicial punishment in 1948, flogging in the army and navy in the 1950s, corporal punishment in prisons and borstals in 1967. Such, however, was the passionate defence of the right to beat children in schools by most teacher unions and successive governments right into the 1980s, that it is most unlikely that pupils would have followed prisoners, soldiers and sailors in gaining protection from corporal punishment without the involvement of the European Court of Human Rights.

That involvement began in 1976 when two Scottish mothers made an application to the European Commission, alleging that the use of corporal punishment in schools attended by their sons was contrary to Article 3 of the European Human Rights Convention ('No-one shall be subjected to torture or to inhuman or degrading treatment or punishment'), and that the government had also failed to respect their parental right, under Article 2 of Protocol 1, to ensure that education and teaching were in line with their 'religious and philosophical convictions'.

Because neither boy had actually received corporal punishment, the Commission and Court found no breach of Article 3. The Court did rule, however, in 1982 that Article 2 of Protocol 1 had been breached because the parents' objections to corporal punishment had not been respected.[8]

In the same year, the Human Rights Committee of the UN, which over-sees implementation of the International Covenant on Civil and Political Rights, decided that Article 7 of that Covenant, which also bars 'inhuman and degrading treatment or punishment', did cover corporal punishment 'including excessive chastisement as an educational or disci-plinary measure'.[9] Ten years later, the Human Rights Committee re-emphasised this, underlining that Article 7 protects, in particular, chil-dren and pupils.[10] Even at this sophisticated level of human rights experts, one notes, however, the distinction in protection offered to chil-dren, who are only to be protected from 'excessive' chastisement.

It is significant that the European Court judgment did not uphold chil-dren's rights to physical integrity, but parents' rights to choose not to have their children beaten. The government, keen as ever to take the absolute minimum action to fulfil its international human rights obliga-tions, waited three years and then tried to introduce a Bill that would enable parents to opt into, or out of, school corporal punishment. By now, however, the teachers' organisations had seen the writing on the wall, and turned to accept full abolition. The Bill was thrown out, and in 1986 the government allowed a free vote on abolition. Against the strongly expressed advice of ministers, the House of Commons deter-mined, by a majority of just one, that all pupils in state-supported edu-cation would be protected from corporal punishment from August 1987.

Grudging to the last, abolition did not cover pupils paid for by their parents in fee-paying schools. The government still maintains in 1994 that parents must be free to pay to have their children beaten in those independent schools that still wish to offer the service, although in response to pressure to extend abolition to cover the whole of the private sector during the passage of the 1993 Education Bill, the government did agree to include a new provision insisting that any corporal punishment administered must not be 'inhuman or degrading'.[11] The law does not provide children who are assaulted in schools with the same protection as assaulted adults: it removes teachers' defence of 'reasonable chastise-ment' in civil proceedings, but leaves the defence intact in criminal pro-ceedings. In other words, a teacher can be sued for damages in a civil court for using any form of corporal punishment, but cannot be prosecuted successfully in a criminal court unless the punishment goes beyond the court's view of 'reasonable'.[12]

CHILDREN ACT PROGRESS

Abolition of school corporal punishment, however incomplete, represented a watershed for children; the Department of Health, which had been waiting for some movement from the Department for Education before barring corporal punishment in children's homes, now extended protection. Using regulations and guidance issued under the Children Act 1989, the Department has implemented its policy that 'outside of the family, physical punishment has no place in the child care environment'.[13] The Act came into effect in October 1991, and has effectively ended physical punishment in all children's homes (including private ones), in local authority and private foster care, and in all group day care including childminding.

Small-scale signs of a low-level judicial rebellion against the policy were seen in 1993, when magistrates in the London Borough of Sutton upheld an appeal by a childminder against a decision of the authority not to register her because she would not guarantee not to smack a minded child.[14] The authority was clearly following government guidance which, issued under the Local Authority Social Services Act 1970, has significant legal status.[15] The childminder wished to follow the pro-smacking views of the parent of the minded child. Sections of the media treated the childminder as a martyr for common sense; a more logical society would have regarded the 4-year-old whom she minds as the true martyr of the piece. The High Court has confirmed the decision of the magistrates.

So that is where we are now. We have almost ended institutional beating of children; we may soon end it altogether where the state is involved in approving and registering substitute carers, but we continue to tolerate parents and other informal carers smacking and even beating and belting their children, and rich parents paying teachers to do it for them.

There is light at the end of the tunnel for children. It comes in another international human rights instrument, and in time it will undoubtedly lead to full recognition of children's equal right to physical and personal integrity.

THE UN CONVENTION

The United Nations Convention on the Rights of the Child was adopted by the General Assembly in November 1989. It has now been ratified – fully accepted – by 154 states around the world. The United Kingdom ratified, a little late, in December 1991. Ratification implies an obligation to implement fully the Convention and to report, two years after ratification and then every five years, to a UN Committee on the Rights of the Child (an elected committee of ten experts).[16] The Convention provides the first set of principles and detailed standards for treatment of children the world over. It clearly upholds children's full right to physical and personal integrity. The preamble refers to the 'equal and inalienable rights of all members of the human family', as well as to children's rights to 'special care and assistance'.

Article 2 states that the rights in the Convention must be available 'without discrimination of any kind, irrespective of the child's or his or her parent's or legal guardian's race, colour, sex, language, religion, political or other opinion, national, ethnic or social origin, property, disability, birth or other status'.

Article 3 provides that in all actions concerning children, 'the best interests of the child must be a primary consideration'. A number of other articles are relevant to gross breaches of the child's right to physical integrity: the right to life and maximum development (Article 6), involvement of children in armed conflict (Article 38) and protection from sexual and other exploitation and abduction of children (Articles 34, 35, 36).

It is Article 19 that asserts the child's right to protection from 'all forms of physical or mental violence':

1. State Parties shall take all appropriate legislative, administrative, social and educational measures to protect the child from all forms of physical or mental violence, injury or abuse, neglect or negligent treatment, maltreatment or exploitation including sexual abuse, while in the care of parents, legal guardians or any other person who has the care of the child.

2. Such protective measures should, as appropriate, include effective procedures for the establishment of social programmes to provide necessary support for the child and for those who have the care of the child, as well as for other forms of prevention and for identification, reporting, referral, investigation, treatment, and follow-up of instances of child maltreatment described heretofore, and, as appropriate, for judicial involvement.

Thus Article 19, while including protection from what is commonly defined as 'abuse', goes further in covering 'all forms of physical or mental violence'. And it also goes beyond the prohibition in Article 37 – 'No child shall be subjected to torture or other cruel, inhuman or degrading treatment or punishment' – which reflects provisions in other international instruments, like the European Convention on Human Rights and the International Covenant on Civil and Political Rights, referred to above.

Also relevant to the right to physical integrity in the school context is Article 28(2): 'State Parties shall take all appropriate measures to ensure that school discipline is administered in a manner consistent with the child's human dignity *and in conformity with the present Convention*' – i.e. in conformity with Article 19, without any form of physical or mental violence.

The Convention, reading Article 2 with Article 19, makes clear that the right to protection from all forms of physical or mental violence cannot be diluted by discrimination on grounds of religion, culture, tradition, etc. The religious justification for physical chastisement is alive and much quoted: there are fundamentalist schools in the United Kingdom which promote their use of the 'rod of correction' as a vital part of the curriculum, consistent with the line from Proverbs, 'Spare the rod and spoil the child'. Some books on child-rearing aimed at Christian parents advocate with enthusiasm the use of implements to beat children (there are, of course, many committed Christians who would authoritatively challenge the selective quotations and interpretations which attempt to justify child-beating on biblical grounds). White social workers are sometimes hesitant to challenge heavy physical punishment when they come across it in a black family, perceiving it as a cultural practice. In fact they are promoting a racist stereotype, conveniently forgetting that it is a cultural practice in most white families (and that promotion of physical punishment and humiliation of children in child-rearing and education was a particularly ugly part of the British colonial 'heritage'). Above all, however, they are failing to uphold the child's right to physical integrity irrespective of parents' religion or culture.

The Convention does not allow persisting concepts of original sin, or of parental 'ownership' of children, to dilute children's right to physical integrity any longer. There will, of course, be those who will try to argue that physical punishment, especially when concealed by nice comfortable words like 'smacking' or 'spanking', is not 'any form of violence'. But such hypocritical and illogical views will not prevail over time.

The Convention also demands review and action on other, even more sensitive, cultural and religious traditions: Article 24(3) obliges states 'to take all effective and appropriate measures with a view to abolishing traditional practices prejudicial to the health of children'. This was drafted with particular reference to female circumcision – genital mutilation of girls and young women. In many societies around the world, initiation rites and other practices involve physical and often mental violence too, invading children's physical integrity without their informed consent. Sometimes they are gross, as in the case of genital mutilation; sometimes less so, as with male circumcision, scarring, scratching, piercing, coinrubbing, etc. Questioning all such practices raises delicate and complex issues. Some would suggest that it is the cultural 'right' of the child to be initiated, and point to the serious consequences in some societies of not following tradition.

The UN Committee on the Rights of the Child, appointed under the Convention to monitor progress towards implementation worldwide, has now begun the process of 'auditing' State Parties' initial reports on progress towards implementation. The Convention is not enforceable in the same way as the European Human Rights Convention; aggrieved children cannot make applications alleging breaches. Already, however, the Committee has challenged corporal punishment, with one member stating that it appeared to be 'incompatible with the Convention'.[17] The Committee does not have straightforward legal powers. The significance of the Convention comes from its internationally validated moral authority – its clear confirmation that children have at least as much right to physical and personal integrity as the rest of us. It is this moral authority that gives new strength to campaigners for this most basic children's right.

WORLDWIDE PROGRESS

The major reason for optimism now is the progress there has already been in a small number of countries, even before adoption of the Convention, to uphold children's right to physical and personal integrity unequivocally in the law. Sweden was the first, in 1979, the International Year of the Child. Swedish family law now reads: 'Children are entitled to care, security and a good upbringing. Children are to be treated with respect for their person and individuality and may not be subjected to physical punishment or any other humiliating treatment.'[18] Finland, Denmark and Norway quickly followed with similar reforms, and in 1989 Austria became the fifth European country to prohibit all physical punishment. In 1985, the Committee of Ministers of the Council of Europe had recommended that all member-states should review their law on punishing children, and consider prohibition of physical punishment.[19]

During 1992, the German Minister of Justice committed her country to a similar reform within two years; in the summer of 1993, a Commission on reform of children's law in Poland recommended similar changes; and in July 1993, the Federal Ministry of Justice in Canada announced legal reform and a government-led information campaign on positive forms of discipline without violence. In Africa, the Second African Congress on

Child Abuse, held in Cape Town in September 1993 with over 600 participants covering fifteen countries, resolved unanimously to support moves to eliminate all physical punishment through education and legal reform. In New Zealand, the statutory Commissioner for Children urged the government to repeal the law confirming parents' rights to use 'reasonable chastisement', and launched his own education campaign. He argued:

> Consider the injustice of hitting children. We hit in order to inflict pain. The law does not permit us to inflict pain on anyone other than our children. Floggings of prisoners and in the armed services, the beating of wives and servants are part of an unwanted brutal past. Our laws prohibit us from inflicting pain on animals. Why our children?[20]

SO MUCH TO GAIN ...

The purpose of prohibiting physical punishment and humiliation of children is not to increase prosecution of parents, nor to increase formal interventions in family life, removing more children. As a Swedish official put it:

> By the prohibition of physical punishment, the legislator wanted to show that a child is an independent individual who can command full respect for his or her person, and who should thus have the same protection against physical punishment or violence as we adults see as being totally natural for ourselves.[21]

In Sweden in fourteen years there has been just one prosecution of a parent for what we would term 'ordinary' physical punishment: a father was fined the equivalent of £9 for 'spanking' his 11-year-old son who felt sufficiently aggrieved to report him. The proportion of children taken into compulsory care is significantly lower than in the United Kingdom, and is reducing. Sweden has, over a long period, given priority to children and therefore to state support for parenting. An overall respect for human rights and consistent action against discrimination in Swedish society made legislation underlining children's status as people an inevitable development.

In arguing for a redefinition of child abuse and for child protection work to be built on the child's right to physical and personal integrity, it is important to emphasise that we are not arguing for more prosecutions or interventions in families, for it is most unlikely that they would benefit children. We already know that much intervention in the name of child protection adds further abuse. If we can begin again from a logical base rooted in children's rights, surely there is more hope that child protection services can become genuinely child-centred? The purpose is to get beyond the incomplete concept of child abuse, to uphold the status of the child as a person, to relegate finally to sad history the idea of ownership and absolute rights over children, and to change both attitudes and practice.

The prime motivation for action must be the upholding of a basic human right. In addition, adults around the world have already documented ample evidence to demonstrate beyond doubt that if we can make violence and humiliation unacceptable in child-rearing, we can dramatically reduce levels of all kinds of inter-personal violence. In several countries recently governmental commissions have been set up following alarm at the escalation of all kinds of inter-personal violence. Seeking strategies for reduction or prevention, in each case they have promoted ending the acceptability of physical punishment of children as a vital priority. As an Australian Commission put it: 'The greatest chance we have to prevent violence in society is to raise children who reject violence as a method of problem-solving, who believe in the right of the individual to grow in a safe environment.'[22]

What we need now is an end to individual, collective and governmental hypocrisy in our attitudes to violence and children. There must be a recognition of the conditioning which has allowed us for so long to justify hurting and humiliating children, and action to create a climate in which legal and other reforms to give children the same right to physical and personal integrity that we adults take for granted become a non-controversial imperative.

As Alice Miller has written: 'We don't yet know, above all, what the world might be like if children were to grow up without being subjected to humiliation, if parents would respect them and take them seriously as people.'[23]

REFERENCES

1. Quoted in Blackstone's *Commentaries*, p. 445.
2. *Parliamentary Debates*, 3rd series (1889), vol. 337, cols. 1379–86 and vol. 338, col. 956.
3. Section 1(7), Children and Young Persons Act 1933; s. 12(7), Children and Young Persons (Scotland) Act 1937; s. 20(6), Children and Young Persons (Northern Ireland) Act 1950.
4. Russell, *A Treatise on Crimes and Misdemeanours*, 1st edn (1819), vol. I, p. 863.
5. *R v Hopley* (1860) 2 F & F 202.
6. *B v Harris* (1990) SLT 208.
7. 'Caning Mother Cleared', *Daily Mail*, 4 October 1991; 'Father: Why I beat my sons', *North Avon Evening Post*, 19 March 1993; 'Victory for Mother who Spanked Girl', *Daily Express*, 20 April 1993.
8. European Court of Human Rights Judgment: *Campbell and Cosans v. UK*, Strasbourg, 25 February 1982.
9. UN Human Rights Committee, *Annual Report*, 16th session (1982).
10. UN Human Rights Committee, *Annual Report*, 44th session (1992).
11. Education Act 1993, s. 293 (England and Wales); s. 294 (Scotland).
12. The legislation is contained in the Education (No. 2) Act 1986, s. 47 (England and Wales), s. 48 (Scotland), and the Education (Northern Ireland) Order 1987.
13. Letter from Mrs Virginia Bottomley, Minister for Health, to EPOCH, 1991.
14. Sutton Family Proceedings Court, 8 July 1993.
15. Department of Health, *Family Support, Day Care and Educational Provision for Young Children*, The Children Act 1989 Guidance and Regulations (London, HMSO, 1991).
16. Text of the UN Convention can be obtained by sending an A4 stamped addressed envelope to the Children's Rights Development Unit, 235 Shaftesbury Avenue, London WC2H 8EL.
17. UN Committee on the Rights of the Child, consideration of initial report from Sudan, press release HR/3298, 27 January 1993.
18. Swedish Parenthood and Guardianship Code, ch. 6, section 1.
19. Council of Europe Committee of Ministers, Recommendation R85/4 on *Violence in the Family*.
20. Ian Hassall, New Zealand Commissioner for Children, Wellington NZ, 1993.
21. Bertil Ekdahl, Swedish Ministry of Justice official, Stockholm, 1979.
22. National Committee on Violence, Australia, 1989. Other governmental bodies that have recommended ending physical punishment of children include the Governmental Commission on 'Prevention and Control of Violence', West Germany, 1990, and the US Surgeon-General's 'Workshop on Violence and Public Health', 1985.
23. Alice Miller, *For Your Own Good: The Roots of Violence in Child-rearing*, (London, Virago, 1987).

7

Munchausen Syndrome by Proxy

Professor Roy Meadow

The term 'Munchausen Syndrome by Proxy' was proposed in 1977 to describe situations in which a person came to be regarded as ill as a result of a false illness story being presented, on their behalf, by another person.[1] Although there are examples of elderly, mentally handicapped and other incapacitated persons suffering Munchausen Syndrome by Proxy abuse, the main use of the term has remained, where it started, with children. The term is used when fabricated illness of children meets the following criteria:

1. Illness in a child which is fabricated by a parent or someone who is in loco parentis.

2. The child is presented for, or requires, medical assessment and care, usually repetitively or persistently. This often results in multiple medical procedures.

3. The perpetrator denies causing the child's illness.

4. Acute symptoms and signs of illness cease when the child is separated from the perpetrator.

The term is a cumbersome one which, although successful in a journalistic sense in alerting clinicians to this form of child abuse, sometimes has been the source of confusion. Some authorities now prefer the term 'Factitious Illness by Proxy'.

The term 'Munchausen Syndrome' was proposed by the late Dr Richard Asher, a London physician, in an article for *The Lancet*:

> Here is described a common syndrome which most doctors have seen, but about which little has been written. Like the famous Baron von Munchausen, the persons affected have always travelled widely; and their stories, like those attributed to him, are both dramatic and untruthful. Accordingly the syndrome is respectfully dedicated to the Baron and named after him.[2]

The label tends to be applied to adults with gross somatisation disorder who relate dramatic and false stories of personal illness. It also tends to be applied more to persons who wander from hospital to hospital with their false stories, and more often to men than to women. The abnormal illness behaviour is at one end of an easily recognisable spectrum. The ways in which persons respond to illness vary greatly, and include many who imagine themselves to be iller than they are, many who exaggerate symptoms and, as a result, gain extra help or comfort from their families or the medical services, as well as others who deliberately invent illness for financial or personal gain (malingering). Those with extremely abnormal illness behaviour, who can be classified as having factitious disorder with physical symptoms (Munchausen Syndrome), are not thought to relish the unpleasant investigations, treatments or surgery that they may receive, but they are thought to enjoy, and have a need for, care and concern from the people and the services to which their 'illness' leads them. In Munchausen Syndrome by Proxy the false illness is invented by another person (i.e. a proxy).

The potential consequences for children who have false illness imposed upon them are as follows:

1. They incur many needless and, at times, harmful investigations and treatments.

2. Genuine disease or injury may be induced by the perpetrator's actions. In extreme cases this may extend to death, for example when a mother partially suffocates her child, trying to cause the child to be unconscious, but smothers the child for too long, thereby causing brain damage or death.

3. They may grow up to be chronic individuals, the child believing the illness story and their inability to participate in normal activities and to attend school or work.

4. They may develop Munchausen Syndrome itself, the child gradually taking over the false illness story from the mother during childhood, and persisting with and embellishing it as an adult.

GUIDELINES

Current guidelines are that Munchausen Syndrome by Proxy abuse should be considered in the category 'physical abuse' when the child is placed on the Child Protection Register. In some ways this is misleading because, although there often is indirect physical abuse and sometimes direct physical abuse of great severity, there is always emotional abuse. Quite often the identified physical abuse – for instance, a single episode of overdosing with prescribed drugs – may represent much less risk to one child than the prolonged emotional abuse of a false illness story for another child. One of the problems for those investigating Munchausen Syndrome by Proxy abuse is that it may be much easier to prove a case of poisoning in court, because of the toxicological evidence, than it is to prove a case of abuse where the mother has merely invented false illness stories or fabricated samples for investigation.

It is helpful to consider Munchausen Syndrome by Proxy abuse as one end of the spectrum of ways in which parents behave when their child is ill.[3] Normal anxious parents worry about their children when they are ill. Those who are particularly anxious, lonely or in difficult circumstances, may worry more and will use their doctor more. Some will perceive symptoms that others do not observe. Others, under greater stress, may exaggerate some of the symptoms to try to gain more help. Many parents who do not gain the help they need from one doctor will take the child to a succession of other doctors. Similarly when a child has genuine illness, some parents will be much more cautious than others in the way they treat that child, and will be over-protective; they needlessly prolong the extent of the child's illness. These are natural ways for parents to behave and health services have a duty to be able to respond to the many different ways in which parents in different societies cope with ill children. It is only when the degree of exaggeration or deception is extreme and positively harmful to the child that it should be classified as abuse.

Some parents abuse their child merely by relating a false illness story over a period of years – for instance, of frequent seizures, so causing their child to have many investigations, prolonged courses of anticonvulsant drugs, and restricted activity.[4] Other parents will supplement their false illness story by fabricating samples (adding chemicals to their child's urine sample; using their own blood or that from meat, smeared around the child's mouth or vulva or mixed in vomit, to simulate bleeding). Others cause direct injury to the child by applying caustic solutions to the skin to cause blistering rashes, smothering the child to cause unconsciousness or seizures, or giving drugs to cause vomiting, diarrhoea or drowsiness.[5] For many mothers it seems to be a progression: they start off with a false illness story and then, after a period of time, raise the stakes and seek to impress the doctors even more by falsifying samples or causing the child to be genuinely ill or injured.

Different authorities include different aspects of parental behaviour in the spectrum of Munchausen Syndrome by Proxy abuse. Most exclude the false accusations of sexual abuse that partners may make against each other at the time of marriage break-up and during custody disputes. Nevertheless, at times, false accusations of sexual abuse (and physical abuse) do fit firmly into the Munchausen Syndrome by Proxy spectrum. Families are recorded in which the mother has made elaborate accusations of sexual abuse by someone outside the family, and has coached the child to provide impressive disclosure detail, as well as injuring the child to fabricate the signs of sexual abuse. Some of the children and their siblings have also suffered factitious illness. For these children, the false sexual abuse is just one of several false illness/health allegations.[6]

A common difficulty for the investigator is that many of the abused children will have had genuine illnesses as well as the suspected fabricated illnesses. Some perpetrating mothers appear to start fabricating illness as a result of the experience of their child having a genuine illness episode. Thus, in cases of factitious epilepsy, it is not uncommon to discover that the child has had one or two genuine seizures, but that the mother has then invented or caused a large number of extra seizures.[7]

The victims tend to be young children and the usual age of onset is under the age of 2. It is unusual for the abuse to start after the age of 8, partly because children are independent enough to give their own story to the doctors. However, children for whom fabricated illness is invented early in life may progress to participate in the deception as they reach school age – some mothers teach the child to trick the doctors and lie.

THE PERPETRATOR

From experience of more than 300 cases, as well as from the cases reported in the medical literature, it is clear that the child's natural mother is the usual perpetrator. My experience is that it is the child's natural mother in 90 per cent of cases, the father in 5 per cent and another carer (for instance, a nurse or childminder) in 5 per cent. The perpetrators rarely have identifiable or treatable mental illness. However, most have personality disorders. As with other forms of child abuse, about a third have suffered definite abuse themselves, most often emotional abuse associated with a lack of love and respect from their own mothers. Rather more than one-quarter of the mothers have abnormal illness behaviour (somatoform disorders) themselves, which for many can be classified as Munchausen Syndrome. Another subgroup of perpetrating mothers indulge in extravagant lies in relation to most aspects of their life.[8,9] The male perpetrators whom I have encountered have been similar to that group of mothers: they tend to deceive their wives and families about their work and lives and extend that exaggeration and fabrication to their children. They have lied about their school achievements, their sporting achievements, their past and their present life. It is common for them to be keen on first aid and to be volunteer ambulance men or firemen. They revel in having their child suffering life-threatening illnesses and in their role as resuscitators; they are altogether smarter than their female partners.

On the whole, personalities stay with us for life. Our personalities may mature and the expression of our personality, in terms of our actions, is modified by changes in our surroundings and in our lifestyle. Nevertheless our personality traits tend to remain with us. This has considerable implications for treatment and prognosis.

Generally the spouse is unaware of what is happening and does not believe it to be possible even when confronted with the facts. Complicity is extremely rare, but the lack of involvement and support from many fathers can, at times, be regarded as passive collusion, somewhat similar to the role that mothers sometimes have in relation to sexual abuse of their children by a male partner. The marriages tend to be ill assorted, either with the perpetrating mother being stronger, more able and more socially aware than her rather ineffectual partner, or alternatively having a somewhat macho partner who goes about his own life without offering appropriate support for her and the children.[10]

CO-MORBIDITY

In common with most forms of child abuse, there is considerable co-morbidity. One extensive study showed that in addition to the Munchausen Syndrome by Proxy abuse, over 70 per cent of the children had suffered other abuse including non-accidental injury, neglect or inappropriate medication.[11] Although many of their brothers and sisters appeared healthy and well cared for, over one-third of the siblings themselves were victims of Munchausen Syndrome by Proxy abuse and nearly a third had either died unexpectedly in early life or were subject to another form of child abuse.[12] This has major implications for childcare proceedings in relation to current brothers and sisters as well as to future children for the perpetrator.

CRIMINAL PROCEEDINGS

The vigour with which criminal proceedings have been pursued varies greatly in different countries, and in the United Kingdom seems to vary according to the sex and circumstances of the perpetrator. My impression is that most perpetrators are not prosecuted. There are obvious difficulties in amassing evidence that is sufficiently robust to achieve a successful criminal prosecution, particularly bearing in mind that the victims are usually too young to give evidence. Regardless of the home circumstances, the quality of parenting, the duration of the abuse or the effect of it on the child, the Crown Prosecution Service seems more likely to prosecute if a child has been given excess drugs or has been smothered. Even when mothers are found guilty of administering poison to their young child, or have deliberately smothered their child, and even when death has resulted, it has been most unusual for the mother to be given a custodial sentence. Usually there is a suspended sentence. Male perpetrators in Britain appear to be treated very differently by the police and the courts. They seem to be regarded as a danger to society and as if they are likely to rampage through the neighbourhood killing children. They tend to be locked up until they appear in court and then to receive long custodial sentences. In general, persons who commit Munchausen Syndrome by Proxy abuse do not harm children other than their own. Nevertheless, because a small minority have harmed other children, one must advise childcare agencies to ensure that someone who has perpetrated Munchausen Syndrome by Proxy should not be put in a position where they are responsible for the care of other children.

The publicity given to the actions of Nurse Beverley Allitt (found guilty in 1993 of four murders, three attempted murders and six charges of bodily harm which she committed on children while working as a nurse on the paediatric ward at Grantham) has drawn attention to the way in which one person may harm many children.[13] The press was correct to describe this as Munchausen Syndrome by Proxy abuse of children for the diagnostic criteria outlined earlier were fulfilled: when working as a nurse for the children she was in loco parentis, and she poisoned and otherwise harmed children, repetitively causing them to be presented as ill; at times, the repetitive actions led to particular children being seriously ill or killed. She presented the children to other colleagues, including the doctors, as if they were ill and denied having any causal role. Her own health record revealed that she had gross personal illness disorder which could be classified as Munchausen Syndrome. However, it was wrong, as the media tended to report, to claim that Nurse Allitt 'had Munchausen Syndrome by Proxy'. It is the children in Grantham who suffered Munchausen Syndrome by Proxy abuse; the term should be used to describe that sort of abuse of children and should not be transferred to the perpetrator (any more than one would suggest that a stepfather who has sexually abused a young girl is himself suffering from sexual abuse).

CHILDCARE PROCEEDINGS

Most cases of Munchausen Syndrome by Proxy abuse are dealt with in family proceedings. There it is probably wisest to avoid too much generalisation concerning Munchausen Syndrome by Proxy and to concentrate on the actual harm done to the child. Each case has to be considered on its own merits and it is important to bear in mind the broad spectrum of behaviour in which different parents cope with illness in their child. Just because a parent has deceived doctors or lied about their child's health does not mean that the child has been severely abused. Cases can be difficult for social services and local authority legal departments because the initial priority is to confirm or reject the probability of fabricated illness. Thus there is a difficult medical diagnosis to be made which, at times, will be the subject of conflicting specialist opinions.[14] Moreover specialists who have been involved with the child's care in the preceding years, and have been tricked by the perpetrating mother into making false diagnoses of genuine illness and organising inappropriate treatment, vary in the speed with which they are willing to acknowledge their past mistakes. It is important to recognise that the severity of the abuse is not related merely to the identified abusive action, but to consider the significance of the abuse in terms of the future parenting for the child. Identified physical abuse may be a small part of much more important emotional abuse. The likelihood of future physical or psychological harm to the child is the next priority and depends on many different factors, particularly a prediction of the future behaviour of the perpetrator.

In general the perpetrators are abusing the child for personal gain. Some mothers merely wish to get the child off their hands and into hospital, looked after by someone else. For others the hospital admission and contact with doctors provide for the mother a haven and a source of comfort, and they are able to close their eyes and their minds to the ensuing suffering that they are causing their child. They fail in the prime duty of all parents: to put their children's needs first. Others have mixed feelings about their child which, at times, amounts to hatred, and their actions on behalf of, or directly to, the child include an element of hatred and aggression.

CONSIDERATION IN RELATION TO FAMILY PROCEEDINGS

The risk of continued abuse is difficult to assess, and many of the considerations are common to other forms of child abuse.[15] They relate to the age and vulnerability of the child, the certainty that abuse has occurred and the degree of its severity, as well as the feasibility of social workers and other therapists working with the perpetrator. I am frequently asked if the perpetrator, usually the child's mother, can be 'treated'. Although she may not have a treatable mental illness, and although she may have definite personality disorder, there may be ways of helping her to become a safer person with her own children. Some of the factors influencing the prospect for change include the following:

1. Her response following confrontation. If the perpetrator can talk openly about what she has done, and be directed to understanding why she acted in that way, the therapist has some hope. However, it is extremely difficult to help mothers who, in the face of overwhelming evidence, deny having injured the child or claim that they can remember none of the details. One of the unfortunate consequences of criminal proceedings is that they tend to encourage the perpetrator to deny the abuse and also encourage the relatives to deny the possibility that one of their family has abused the child. Moreover, criminal proceedings tend to take priority and prevent proper and urgent consideration being given to the needs of the child. The mother is more likely to talk about her feelings and her circumstances if other family members accept what she has done (it is much more helpful if they say 'I know what you've done and it was wrong, but I still love you', than if they say 'I love you and I know you would never have done anything like that').

2. The perpetrator's personality. That minority of mothers who themselves have gross somatisation disorder, particularly when it amounts to flamboyant Munchausen Syndrome, are particularly difficult to help. They have immense personal needs, and tend to be unreliable and unable to change their behaviour. Those with addic-

tion to drugs or alcohol pose additional problems. A long history of self-harm, eating disorders or anti-social behaviour, including arson and other criminal acts, are unfavourable factors.

3. The mother's relationship with the child and her capacity to accept, love and give priority to the child.

4. Family circumstances. Perpetrators may be helped when they have strong family support in the neighbourhood, particularly people who will be kind and motherly to them. Assessment of the marriage is much more problematic; many of the perpetrators have partners who seem unsupportive. Although the perpetrator may claim great love for their partner, several of them have led a better life when their marriage has broken up and particularly if they have found a new partner.

5. Life situation. Many of the perpetrators feel worthless and, if they find worthwhile employment or a useful role outside the home, achieve considerable personal fulfilment which enables them to alter their behaviour and be a satisfactory parent.

OUTCOME

Relatively little has been published about the long-term outcome for these children. As would be expected, there has been a tendency for children who have been repetitively suffocated, or who have been poisoned, or injured in a family in which a previous child has died unexpectedly, to be placed in long-term alternative care at an early stage. Thus it is not possible to assess the outcome of comparable children who have been left with their natural family as opposed to those who have been removed from it. In some ways the literature gives a rather misleading impression in terms of future mortality. Our experience has been that it is extremely rare for a child who has been dealt with through standard childcare procedures to incur permanent physical damage or fatal injury following childcare proceedings which have restored the child to the perpetrating mother. Nevertheless there is a worrying morbidity.[16] Of fifty-four index children followed up for two to fourteen years, nearly half had continuing problems of one sort or another and an outcome that was rated as poor. Nine of the children were subject to further fabrications, despite the previous proceedings and the established supervisory arrangements. There were considerable psychological and behavioural problems, including conduct disorder and school problems, for both the index children and their brothers and sisters. The central role of child protection agencies working together with paediatric and mental health services has to be maintained over a long time, continuing through the school years and certainly until the child is at least 8. Supervision has to be controlled and must be able to cope with the mother (and child) changing their family name, their health advisers and moving to other parts of the country.

When children are older the abuse is more difficult to deal with, partly because of the long attachment that the child will have to the perpetrating parent. Even more alarming (and more difficult to deal with because of legislation) are young adults and sometimes older ones, who are still having factitious illness imposed on them by parents. (It is a reminder that childhood does not stop at any legally defined age of 16 or 18 years; childhood stops when your parents die.)

If it is decided that the child can stay with, or be returned to, the abusing mother, long-term follow-up is essential and ideally it should be from someone who has been involved with the initial abuse. It is difficult for successive agencies or doctors to appreciate the nature of the previous abuse or its potential severity and danger; it is also difficult for them to establish a satisfactory relationship with the mother. Commonly the mother may feel antagonism to the doctor, health visitor or social worker who has detected the abuse. Yet at the same time the mother usually has more respect for the person who has arrived at the right diagnosis than for those who have been muddling along for several years, failing to realise what is happening. The person who has detected the abuse, or who has been involved with the disclosure work, and knows the mother and the circumstances, is likely to be in the best position to detect further abuse and also to talk freely with, and help, the mother in the future.

REFERENCES

1. R. Meadow, 'Munchausen Syndrome by Proxy: The hinterland of child abuse', *Lancet* 2 (1977), pp. 343–5.

2. R. Asher, 'Munchausen's Syndrome', *Lancet* 1 (1951), pp. 339–41.

3. R. Meadow, 'Factitious Illness: The hinterland of child abuse', in *Recent Advances in Paediatrics*, No 7 (Edinburgh, Churchill Livingstone, 1984), pp. 217–32.

4. R. Meadow, 'Fictitious Epilepsy', *Lancet* 2 (1984), pp. 25–8.

5. R. Meadow, 'Munchausen Syndrome by Proxy', *Archives of Disease in Childhood*, 57 (1982), pp. 92–8; D. A. Rosenberg, 'Web of Deceit: A literature review of Munchausen Syndrome by Proxy', *Child Abuse and Neglect*, 11 (1987), pp. 547–63; R. Meadow, 'Suffocation, Recurrent Apnea, and Sudden Infant Death', *Journal of Paediatrics*, 117 (1990), pp. 351–7; M. P. Samuels, W. McClaughlin, R. R. Jacobson, C. F. Poets and D. P. Southall, 'Fourteen Cases of Imposed Upper Airway Obstruction', *Archives of Disease in Childhood*, 67 (1992), pp. 162–70.

6. R. Meadow, 'False Allegations of Abuse and Munchausen Syndrome by Proxy', *Archives of Disease in Childhood*, 68 (1993), pp. 444–7.

7. *Op. cit.* (n. 4).

8. C. Bools, B. Neale and R. Meadow, 'Munchausen Syndrome by Proxy: A study of psychopathology', *Child Abuse and Neglect* (1994, forthcoming).

9. H. A. Schreier and J. A. Libow, *Hurting for Love (Munchausen by Proxy Syndrome)* (Guilford Press, 1993).

10. *Op. cit.* (n. 8).

11. C. N. Bools, B. Neale and S. R. Meadow, 'Co-morbidity Associated with Fabricated Illness (Munchausen Syndrome by Proxy)', *Archives of Disease in Childhood*, 67 (1992), pp. 77–9.

12. *Ibid.*

13. N. Davies, *Murder on Ward 4* (Chatto and Windus, 1993).

14. G. Lyons, 'Munchausen Syndrome by Proxy', *New Law Journal* (9 July 1993), pp. 988–90.

15. D. A. Waller, 'Obstacles to the Treatment of Munchausen by Proxy Syndrome', *Journal of the American Academy of Child Psychology*, 22 (1983), pp. 80–5; B. Neale, C. N. Bools and R. Meadow, 'Problems in the Assessment and Management of Munchausen Syndrome by Proxy Abuse', *Children and Society*, 5 (1991), pp. 324–33.

16. C. N. Bools, B. Neale and S. R. Meadow, 'Follow up of Victims of Fabricated Illness (Munchausen Syndrome by Proxy)', *Archives of Disease in Childhood*, 69 (1993), pp. 625–30.

8

Allegations of Child Abuse: the Role of the Medical Examiner

Dr Peter Dean
*Forensic Medical Examiner
and HM Coroner*

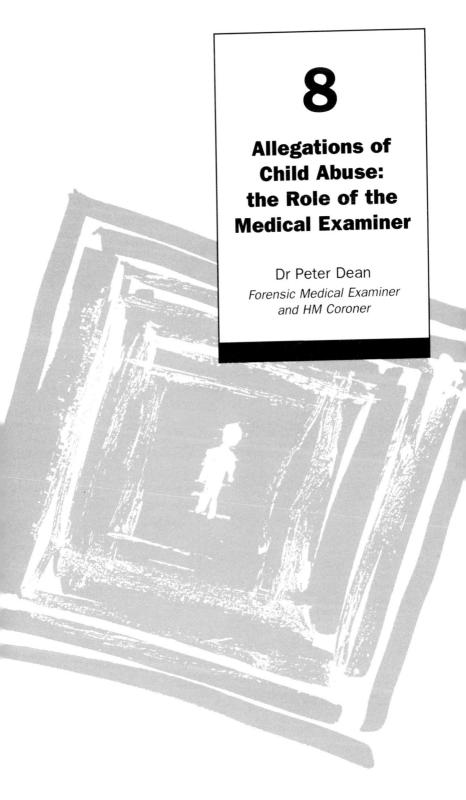

In dealing with any allegation of assault, whether physical or sexual in nature, the medical practitioner assumes certain responsibilities over and above those duties normally arising from the day-to-day care of one's patients. In addition to those duties which are essentially therapeutic in nature, one is also gathering and assessing evidence which may be of importance in confirming or refuting allegations that have been made.

For this reason, one can not over-emphasise the need for the medical examiner to remain impartial and objective at all times, and, particularly where allegations of child abuse are concerned, to realise that he or she is functioning not in isolation, but as one member of a multidisciplinary team, whose evidence may be of no greater or lesser importance than that of any other member of the team.

Problems often arise from the mistaken, yet still widely held, belief that the medical examination on its own will provide the answer as to whether sexual abuse has occurred. Sadly, such expectations may at best disappoint, and at worst lead to miscarriages of justice and consequent untold damage to those children and families concerned.

Although the medical examination can be of considerable benefit in recording any abnormal findings, taking forensic and bacteriological samples, treating any complications or medical problems, and reassuring the child and the family, in many cases where sexual abuse has occurred there may be no physical findings of any significance at all on examination. It is also equally important to appreciate that many of the physical findings that have been associated with abuse may also have perfectly innocent alternative explanations. For this reason, it is clear that there must be an absence of bias, prejudice and dogma not only in one's approach to the clinical examination itself, but also in the subsequent presentation of any clinical evidence in court.

Problems will inevitably arise when doctors disagree in their interpretation of the clinical findings. Useful guidance, however, is given in the *Recommendations of the Report of the Inquiry into Child Abuse in Cleveland (1987)*, one of which advises that:

Medical practitioners who have examined a child for suspected sexual abuse and disagree in their findings and conclusions should discuss their reports and resolve their differences where possible; in the absence of agreement identify the areas of dispute, recognising their purpose is to act in the best interests of the child.[1]

THE MEDICAL WITNESS

One ever-present danger of the adversarial process is the risk that witnesses will become partisan in the presentation of their evidence to the court. The medical witness, whether professional or expert, must remember at all times that he or she is there as a witness to the court, in order to assist the court as a whole rather than one party in particular.

The provision of medical reports and statements should always be approached in the same manner, and reports must be written in the same clear unbiased way, recognising the requirement to tell not just the truth, but the whole truth.

The medical witness who attempts to support one side of the case by omitting or failing to emphasise findings that support the 'opposing' side, creates a situation where miscarriages of justice are likely, and runs the risk of being exposed and discredited in court when subjected to cross-examination and when notes are inspected. By choosing to be selective in what is included in the report, the medical witness will also have failed to advise fully and assist counsel preparing the case in assessing the relative strengths, weaknesses and problems that may be encountered.

THE NATURE OF ABUSE

Abuse itself may take many different forms and present in many different ways. It may be primarily physical or primarily sexual in nature, but also includes those children who fail to thrive because of neglect or emotional abuse.[2] Sexual abuse itself covers a wide range of different offences, ranging from acts of penetrative sexual intercourse, either anal, vaginal or oral; fondling or other indecent and inappropriate contact, either by the offender on the child or vice versa; through to involving children in various forms of pornography.

The presentation will depend on the form, extent and severity of the abuse, the age and sex of the child, the history of any previous abuse, the relationship to the abuser, and any relevant family dynamics and relationships. The victim may be male or female, and there is growing awareness that abusers, physical or sexual, may be male or female. Contrary to the widely held public image of child abuse being perpetrated by strangers in some public place, the majority of sexual abusers are known to the child, and the abuse takes place in a familiar or domestic environment.

The abuser in these circumstances operates in a manner designed to avoid detection and to prolong the opportunity for the abuse to continue. It is likely to be subtle and covert, starting in a less intrusive manner and escalating as time goes on. This form of ongoing chronic child sexual abuse is less likely to be accompanied by the more clear-cut, acute and more diagnostic signs found in the rarer situation of the single violent assault by a stranger. It is important to bear this in mind when interpreting the physical findings on examination, and it is also important that this is considered when an examination is planned after the initial suspicion of abuse has been raised.

EXAMINATION

In the great majority of cases, where the abuse is thought to be chronic and ongoing, there is no need for the examination to be conducted as an emergency procedure. It is always far more important to ensure that every examination is conducted in appropriate circumstances by suitably trained, forensically aware, experienced and sympathetic doctors, rather than in an atmosphere of haste and anxiety by the first medically qualified person available.

Where an acute incident appears to have taken place, it is clearly important that the examination does take place at the earliest possible opportunity, so that any injuries can be documented and treated promptly, any necessary forensic samples can be taken while still fresh and likely to be of assistance, and the opportunity taken to provide early diagnosis and treatment of sexually transmitted disease, and post-coital contraception where appropriate.

No matter how acute the circumstances, the same high standards of medical care, compassion and objectivity must be maintained, and the interests of the child must be paramount at all times.

Valid and appropriate consent must be obtained and recorded prior to the commencement of any examination. This should also be sought from the child, as well as from a person with parental responsibility, if the child is of sufficient age and understanding. Consent should also cover the passage of any necessary information and samples to police and social services for use in connection with possible court proceedings, and the consent form currently in use in the Metropolitan Police Area covers these and other important points.

Any victim of a sexual assault will have experienced a potentially devastating situation over which they have had no control, and it is of paramount importance that the patient in this situation, child or adult, does have that control where the medical examination is concerned, if it is not to be perceived as yet another assault.

For the child, agreement should be reached that if at any time they want the examination to stop, they need only to put their hand up, as if at school, or say 'stop', and the examination will stop straight away. This can be rehearsed a few times with the child, and time spent doing this, as well as time spent talking about school, hobbies, favourite lessons, toys, games and pastimes, will prove invaluable in building a rapport with the child, and lessening the negative or worrying aspects of an examination. It goes without saying, of course, that any such agreement to stop at the child's request must be respected and rigidly adhered to, should the child so signal.

History

Prior to the examination, a history of the alleged incident or incidents will have been given, usually by a parent, social worker or police child protection officer, in order that the examination can be properly directed to all of the relevant areas. If further information is required from the child at this time, it is important that no leading questions are asked, and no question or comment phrased in such a way as to raise the possibility later that ideas and allegations could have been put into the child's head by inappropriate questioning.

The history of the incident should include the nature of the alleged abuse, whether restraint or physical violence was used and in what form, the number of episodes (and number of abusers if more than one), and the location of the alleged incident – particularly important in stranger abuse where there may be injuries from the terrain or signs of local vegetation caught in clothes or hair.

In addition to the history of the incident itself, any medical examination must be preceded by a history of the child's general health, with specific inquiry into any skin problems, constipation, diarrhoea, incontinence or urinary problems. Changes in school performance, sleep or appetite disturbances, truancy and anti-social, self-harming or sexualised behaviour may all be of importance. Inquiry should also be made, where appropriate, into any history of vaginal soreness or discharge, and any menstrual history and the possible use of internal tampons. Use of the latter is not considered to cause tears, bruises, grazes or significant damage to the hymen, although there may be some slight stretching or increased distensibility.

An assessment should be made as to whether the child's emotional and physical development are appropriate for his or her age, and some record of the child's general behaviour and approach to the prospect of examination may be of assistance.

The initial assessment of the child should include a 'top to toe' examination. This serves to build rapport with the child with a non-threatening, more familiar form of examination, before any attempt at genital examination is conducted. It also provides evidence of any bruises, scratches, grip marks, bites or other wounds which may be of relevance.

Injuries in children should always be considered in the context of the age and state of development of the child. The toddler learning to walk may have 'innocent' bruising from a fall, and bruising on the shins, for example, often occurs during the course of normal play in school-age children. The clinician should consider whether the examination findings are consistent with the history given, and whether there are any other features, such as an incompatible history or unexplained delay in presentation, that would give rise to an increased level of concern. Where circumstances indicate further investigation, a full skeletal X-ray survey may be very revealing in some children.

BRUISING

Bruises, or contusions, which form the basis for much medico-legal debate and argument both in and out of court, result from blood leaking from damaged blood vessels beneath an intact skin, and are commonly, but not exclusively, caused by the application of blunt force. Bruising may also occur around puncture wounds such as injection sites, and may less commonly occur spontaneously, or in response to minimal trauma, in the presence of certain acquired or inherited bleeding disorders. The presence of bleeding tendencies, in cases of repeated unexplained episodes of bruising, can usually be excluded by performing coagulation studies (testing the various components of normal blood clotting) and other blood tests.

The part of the bruise that is visible to the observer represents blood in the tissues, which has leaked from the damaged vessels, viewed through the intact skin and subcutaneous tissues. It may take a period of time for the bruise to be visible to the naked eye as sufficient blood accumulates in the tissues, and in these circumstances bruising may not always be apparent if the examination takes place within a few hours, or even a day, of the injury occurring.

The extent of the bruising will depend on many factors, such as the nature and intensity of the force applied; the age, health and nutritional status of the subject; and the site at which the blow lands. Lax tissues over bony prominences bruise particularly easily.

Bruising may appear to shift or track through tissue planes under gravitational effects, and can, therefore, appear at a site remote from where the actual force was applied. This is different from the position of an abrasion or laceration, which will faithfully record the exact site of impact that caused it.

Ageing of Bruises

The ageing of bruises is a subject that causes much debate, and provides a ready source of problems and pitfalls for the unwary. Bruises go through a series of colour changes as a result of the progressive breakdown and subsequent removal of the pigments that give blood its normal colour. The initial reddening and mauve discoloration will become darker as more blood leaks out of the vessels, and over the next few days, as the pigment breaks down, a greenish hue develops, followed by yellow or yellow-brown discoloration, with coincident fading of the darker colours.

Bruising may last three or four weeks or may have resolved completely in a week and, despite the varied time-scales of colour changes given in different forensic textbooks, the time of appearance of each different colour change cannot be given with any degree of precision in view of the tremendous inter-personal variation. There are profound dangers in over-interpreting what has been found on clinical examination, and a review and study of colour changes with time, conducted by Langlois and Gresham in 1991, suggested that 'it was only possible to conclude that a bruise with a yellow colour was more than 18 hours old'.[3]

Bruises of different colours are usually of different ages, but that may not always be the case, as the intensity of colour seen will also depend on the size and density of the bruise. With this caveat in mind, if a child has bruises of the same size and density, but of different colours, one can reasonably deduce that they were inflicted at different times. Under these circumstances one could say, for example, that bruises that are green or brown in colour were inflicted some days before mauve ones. These findings can be extremely significant in cases of alleged physical abuse, where the pattern of injury is often repetitive, and is analogous to finding multiple fractures at different stages of healing on a skeletal X-ray survey.

Various experimental methods have been utilised to attempt to age bruises using light microscopy, enzyme reactions and special staining techniques, but these are not of assistance in the clinical situation. In the most severe cases of abuse where a fatality has occurred, attempting to interpret findings from post-mortem tissue samples can also lead to inaccuracy as, paradoxically, some vital reaction may persist into the early post-mortem period.

After a bruise has resolved and is no longer visible to the naked eye, it may still be possible to visualise and photograph it using an ultraviolet light source. This results from changes in the distribution of the pigment melanin in the skin after injury. Although invisible to the naked eye, the areas with increased pigment absorb more ultraviolet light, whereas the depigmented areas reflect more ultraviolet light. By using this technique, older injuries may be visualised, although it is not always effective, particularly in the first few months after injury. The absence of signs with ultraviolet light does not, therefore, exclude injury having occurred.[4]

ABRASIONS, LACERATIONS AND INCISIONS

In addition to any bruises, the presence and state of healing of any abrasions, lacerations or incised wounds or lacerations should be recorded.

An abrasion, or graze, is an injury that involves the superficial layer of the skin, rather than penetrating its full thickness into the deeper tissues.

Lacerations penetrate and split the full thickness of the skin through to the tissues beneath, and result from force being applied to the soft tissues. They may result particularly from blunt force to the skin over bony prominences, where the edges of the laceration may appear sharper and almost incised on appearance, or from tearing forces, where the edges may appear more ragged. The edges of a laceration may be bruised or abraded, and one may see vessels or nerves running across the base of the split.

An incision, however, is caused by cutting the tissues with a sharp edge or instrument, and may result in considerable bleeding as vessels are cut rather than crushed. The edges have a cleaner appearance than a laceration, without the bruising or abrasion that may be seen on the margin of the latter. The edges and overall character of such injuries should be carefully examined and recorded, as they may provide much useful information relating to the manner in which the injury was caused.

When one examines these areas of injury, whether on general examination or in the genital area, one must consider whether the findings (or lack of them) are consistent with the history that was given, and whether there are any other reasonable or possible explanations.

In addition to 'top to toe' examination of the skin surface, the inside of the mouth should also be carefully examined for signs of disease or injury. Lacerations, a torn fraenum (a fold of skin inside the mouth), broken teeth and bruising on the palate (for example, following oral sex) can all be of significance.

SEXUAL ABUSE

When allegations of sexual abuse have been made, the general examination will be followed by a more detailed inspection of the ano-genital area, and it is this aspect of the examination, and the interpretation of any findings, that has proved to be a continuing source of controversy. In this area in particular, the medical examiner must be aware of the duty to remain impartial and objective at all times, and to avoid the pitfalls of misinterpretation and of over-interpretation.

It is well recognised that trauma from sexual abuse, including acts of vaginal and anal intercourse, can heal completely without leaving any residual physical signs. A normal examination, therefore, does not exclude the possibility of some form of abuse having taken place. It is also essential to note that many of the possible examination findings that can be caused by abuse may also have alternative innocent explanations.

The majority of cases of vulvo-vaginitis, which causes redness, soreness and discharge in young girls, result not from abuse or infection but from a combination of some local irritation and the relatively low oestrogen levels found until endogenous oestrogen production increases as puberty approaches.

The Hymen

There is considerable variation in the appearance of the 'normal' hymen, and these different forms have been described as 'annular', 'crescentic' and 'congenital frilly' or 'fimbriated', with rarer forms such as a 'cribriform' hymen, with multiple small openings, or a 'barred' type, with a residual horizontal or vertical bar or septum of membrane.[5]

The hymen and the size of the hymenal orifice will alter with the age of the child, the state of relaxation of the child, whether gentle labial traction is applied during examination, and the position in which the child is examined.

The size of the hymenal orifice has formed the basis for much discussion, and it has been stated that the transverse diameter from infancy to the age of 4 years is about 4 mm, and after 5 years of age the transverse diameter in millimetres is roughly equal to the child's age, up to approximately 1 cm at puberty.[6] It has been emphasised that the size of the orifice should not be the sole basis for a diagnosis of abuse, but it may be supportive.[7]

Because of the variation in the size of the orifice, not only between different children but also in any one child at different times due to position and state of relaxation, it is preferable to consider and carefully examine the overall appearance and integrity of the surrounding hymenal membrane, rather than making dogmatic pronouncements based on the size of the orifice alone.

One should systematically examine the hymen, looking at its width, to see whether there are any areas where the hymen appears to be narrowed or deficient, possibly indicating repeated, gentle, blunt penetration; looking at the edge, to see if it is thickened or rolled, suggesting similar trauma; looking for defects, particularly if angled, sharp or 'peaked', suggesting previous tears or lacerations; and generally examining for any additional features such as the presence of healed scars, or the exposure of more of the vaginal interior than would normally be seen on examination.

The Colposcope

In some centres in America and Australia the colposcope, a binocular optical instrument which magnifies and illuminates the vaginal area and is normally used in gynaecological practice for the detection and treatment of early cervical cancer, has been used to assist in the examination of children where sexual abuse has been alleged.[8] It also provides an effective means for clinical and evidential photographs to be taken of any findings.

The report of the Royal College of Physicians in 1991 did not, however, recommend a colposcope 'for general use'. It recognised that 'it gives an accurate measurement of the hymenal orifice and can be very helpful in allowing the vascular pattern to be demonstrated' but, because it could reveal minor genital trauma that was not otherwise detected, it cautioned that care was needed in the interpretation of colposcopic findings, as there was 'uncertainty about the incidence of minor findings in a normal population'.[9]

Although used in gynaecological practice, the colposcope is not in common use in the investigation of allegations of child sexual abuse in Britain at the present time. This situation may well change and if it does, high-quality colposcopic photographs of normal and abnormal findings would also have the additional educational benefit of being usable for peer review, and would also provide a useful aid for discussing difficult cases and agreeing on the extent and significance of any clinical findings.

When examining the genital area, the presence of other injuries that suggest the use of force should be noted but, as stated previously, these are more likely to be seen in cases of abuse by a stranger rather than in the familial situation.

The presence of any signs of sexually transmitted disease must also be noted and appropriate management instituted. Any evidence to suggest skin disease that could mimic sexual abuse, for example lichen sclerosus et atrophicus, should be also considered and recorded.[10]

Accidental damage may occur in the genital area, the three most common types of injury being caused by straddling, accidental penetration, and tearing due to forced stretching of the perineum when the legs are suddenly abducted. Accidental injury to the hymen itself, however, is rare.[11] This finding is confirmed by Bays and Chadwick, who stated that 'Accidents, masturbation and use of tampons are very unlikely to cause injury to the hymen or internal genital structures.'[12]

Anal Area

When examining the anal area, as with vaginal examination, it is also the case that intercourse may have taken place without leaving any residual physical signs, and many of the physical signs that can be found after anal intercourse may also occur naturally. McCann et al., in a study of prepubertal children selected for non-abuse, found that perianal erythema was present in 41 per cent; wedge-shaped smooth areas in the midline were present in 26 per cent; 15 per cent had reflex anal dilatation at thirty seconds; and tags or folds were present anteriorly in 11 per cent.[13]

Where anal intercourse has been frequent, a triad of signs has been described consisting of thickening of the skin of the anal verge, with resulting reduction or obliteration of the normal anal skin folds; increased elasticity of the anal sphincter muscles; and reduction in power of the anal sphincter muscles, with a reduced 'anal grip' as a consequence.[14]

The latter two signs can only be tested for if a digital examination is conducted, and whether this should be done or not has also been a subject for debate. It has been argued that a digital examination provides essential information for assessing the presence and extent of any constipation present, which may be of significance if there is any sign of fissures or reflex anal dilatation, but some have argued that it is unnecessarily intrusive, and should not be done. Each case should be considered on its own merits, taking into consideration the nature of the particular allegation, the presence of any other relevant physical findings and, of paramount importance, the best interests of that particular child.

Forensic Samples

Whether forensic samples are taken will also be determined by the circumstances of each particular case. The time since the alleged offence must be considered, taking into account the survival times of spermatozoa and seminal fluid after an incident occurs. Spermatozoa may be detected for up to six days in the vagina, three days in the anus, and twelve to fourteen hours in the mouth. Seminal fluid may be detected for up to twelve to eighteen hours in the vagina, and up to three hours in the anus.[15]

Where forensic samples are taken, and in practice this is only in a minority of cases of alleged child sexual abuse because of the nature of many of the allegations and the time-scales involved, the correct procedures must be always followed. Specimens must always be taken with extreme care. For example, inadvertently contaminating internal swabs with material from outside the entrance to the vagina or anus could have serious legal consequences, suggesting that a more serious offence was committed. Specimens must always be appropriately sealed and labelled, with different doctors seeing the child and the suspected assailant in different places to avoid the possibility of cross-contamination, and the identity of the person to whom any samples are handed must always be recorded, to ensure that the continuity of the evidence can be demonstrated.

It is clear that allegations of physical and sexual abuse present the medical practitioner with a unique, complex and challenging range of problems, requiring a sympathetic yet impartial manner, an open mind and a professional attention to detail. It is hoped that if these standards are met, the best interests of the child, and of all of those touched by these allegations, will be upheld.

REFERENCES

1. *The Report of the Inquiry into Child Abuse in Cleveland (1987)* Cm 412 (London, HMSO), p. 248.
2. A. Levy (ed.), *Focus on Child Abuse*, (London, Hawksmere, 1989), pp. 20–31.
3. N. E. I. Langlois and G. A. Gresham, 'The Ageing of Bruises: A review and study of the colour changes with time', *Forensic Science International*, 50 (1991), pp. 227–38.
4. S. M. Hempling, 'The Applications of Ultraviolet Photography in Clinical Forensic Medicine', *Medicine, Science and the Law*, 21: 3 (1981), pp. 215–22; T. C. Krauss and S. C. Warlen, 'The Forensic Science Use of Reflective Ultraviolet Photography', *Journal of Forensic Sciences*, 30:1 (1985), pp. 262–8.
5. D. Paul, 'The Medical Aspects of the Investigation of Alleged Sexual Abuse in Children', *Medicine, Science and the Law*, 26:2 (1986).
6. *Physical Signs of Sexual Abuse in Children*, A Report of the Royal College of Physicians (1991).
7. *Ibid.*
8. B. A. Woodling and A. Heger, 'The Use of the Colposcope in the Diagnosis of Sexual Abuse in the Paediatric Age Group', *Child Abuse and Neglect*, 10 (1986), pp. 111–14.
9. *Op. cit.* (n. 6).
10. H. B. Kean and M. D. B. Clarke, 'Sexual Assault or Skin Disease?', *The Police Surgeon*, 33 (1988), pp. 6–18; S. E. Handfield-Jones *et al.*, 'Lichen Sclerosus et Atrophicus Misdiagnosed as Sexual Abuse', *British Medical Journal*, 294 (1987), pp. 1404–5.
11. R. West *et al.*, 'Accidental Vulval Injuries in Childhood', *British Medical Journal*, 298 (1989), pp. 1002–3.
12. J. Bays and D. Chadwick, 'Medical Diagnosis of the Sexually Abused Child', *Child Abuse and Neglect*, 17 (1993), pp. 91–110.
13. J. McCann *et al.*, 'Perianal Findings in Prepubertal Children Selected for Non-abuse', *Child Abuse and Neglect*, 13 (1989), pp. 179–93.
14. *Op. cit.* (n. 5).
15. *Op. cit.* (n. 6).

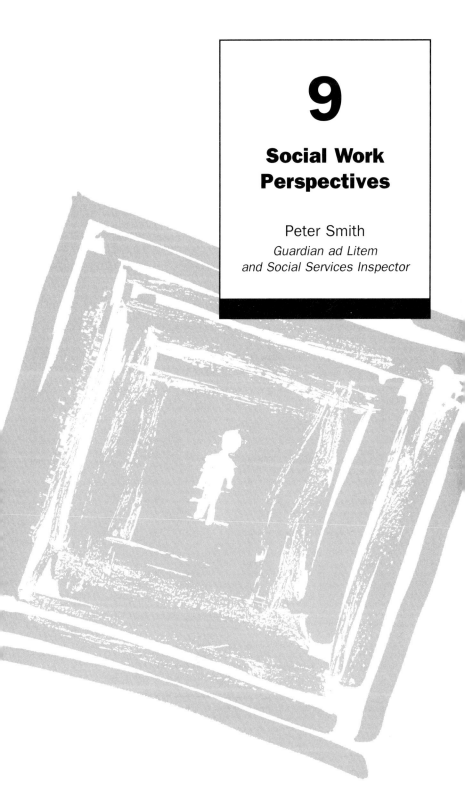

9

Social Work
Perspectives

Peter Smith
Guardian ad Litem
and Social Services Inspector

The Children Act 1989 is the new legal framework for social work with children and families. Of equal importance to the new court orders are the clearer, stronger and more wide-ranging duties on local authorities to provide a range of family support services for children in need. The definition of children in need (s. 17(10)) includes, but is not limited to, children whose health or development is likely to be significantly impaired.

The Children Act is the government's response to widespread criticism of previous legislation from lawyers, social workers, politicians, parents, the European Court of Human Rights and the media. The consensus of approval for the new legislation both in Parliament and in professional circles was remarkable and broadly based. The Act attempts to achieve a fairer balance between the need for state intervention to protect children at risk and parents' rights to legal redress to avoid unwarranted interference in family life. The administrative powers of local authorities have been reduced in favour of judicial scrutiny of decisions regarding, in particular, public law contact arrangements and measures to protect children in an emergency. At the same time as increasing the court's powers in certain respects (there are notable exceptions to the trend), there has been more training and specialisation by magistrates and judges who hear public law children's cases.

This chapter highlights the limitations of present knowledge and the consequential scope for the influence of emotional and highly personal views. It draws on data so far available about public law orders made since the implementation of the Act in October 1991. It cannot be emphasised too strongly that it is too soon to come to any definitive conclusions about the Act's impact on child protection social work. Long-standing questions of social work practice and the underlying moral dilemmas are revisited in the light of newly available information.

SUMMARY OF COURT DATA

It is essential to remember that cases that go to court are a very small percentage of the sum of local authority child protection work. Four per cent of the cases referred to social services departments (SSDs) in one study resulted in court action during the investigation.[1] A comparison of the number of court orders made before and after implementation of the Children Act (see Table 9.1) gives only partial, albeit important, evidence about the impact of the Act on child protection practice.

Table 9.1 Comparison of Estimates of Court Orders Made Pre- and Post-Children Act

	April 1990 to March 1991	October 1991 to September 1992	October 1992 to September 1993*
Place of Safety Order/Emergency Protection Orders	5,000	2,300	2,200
Care Orders	3,300 (CYPA 1969) 2,900 (other legislation, including interim care orders)	1,600	3,000

* These figures are provisional.

With the introduction of major new legislation and consequent changes in the way that data are collected, comparisons of headline figures pre- and post-Children Act must be treated with caution. However, it is clear that the number of care orders and short-term orders to remove children is substantially lower than before the Act.

Theoretical Frameworks

There are broadly three theoretical frameworks that seek to explain the physical and sexual abuse of children.

1. *Individual pathology*. The reasons for child abuse are understood to derive from the personality of the parent, who is therefore examined for characteristics such as lack of impulse control, aggression and a history of experiencing violence as a child.

2. *Family dynamics.* This school of thought looks to an understanding of family interactions to explain abuse and assesses the ability of the parents to take responsibility to change their abusive behaviour.

3. *Social deprivation.* The origins of abusive situations for children are seen in deprived material and social circumstances – for example, poverty and poor housing – which give rise to pressures on parents, increasing the likelihood of the abuse of children.

Some writers[2] have attempted to bring these theories together with an anti-oppressive perspective and taking feminist critiques into account. Each theoretical framework suggests different avenues to explore to understand better any particular abusive situation, and also suggests different courses of action to attempt to safeguard the child. Thus, if deprived social circumstances are seen as causative, a social worker may focus on rehousing a family, ensuring that entitlements to welfare benefits are fully realised and perhaps arranging some form of day care to alleviate the distress associated with looking after children in poor surroundings. If individual pathology is seen as primarily responsible, the social worker may provide or organise counselling or therapy.

In practice social workers mostly recognise that the aetiology of child abuse is complex and that individual, family and social factors are intricately interwoven. All these factors are relevant and should be carefully considered when seeking to understand and to change the circumstances where children are believed to be at risk.

These theoretical frameworks are important in enabling social workers and others to conceptualise the problem, to seek further information and to plan future courses of action. There is a considerable distance between decisions to be made regarding individual children and the theoretical framework. They operate at too high a level of abstraction to indicate authoritatively which children must be removed from their families to ensure their safety or what kind of help will enable which children to remain safely in which families. There is a growing body of research to inform the exercise of professional judgement. But in most situations there is no clearly definable best course of action, no scientifically watertight basis for decisions. There remain broad areas for the exercise of professional discretion. There are many cases, however, where the exercise of professional discretion may appear to parents and others more like the authoritarian exercise of personal prejudice.[3]

INCIDENCE

The understanding of the social problem of child abuse is shaped by moral considerations and emotional responses more than by scientific enquiry and statistical evidence. Child abuse is invariably a private matter, largely inaccessible to researchers for both ethical and practical reasons. Both abusers and victims face frightening disincentives – prison, further beatings, family break-up – to deter honest reporting to outside enquiry. The NSPCC estimated in 1985 that there were 156 child deaths as a result of abuse. In 1991, 318 children under the age of 15 were killed in traffic accidents. Public and media outrage does not seem proportionate to the numbers of children dying from different causes. This is because the public, for impeccably humanitarian reasons, is horrified by the fact of parents causing the deaths of their defenceless children whom they are responsible for protecting and nurturing.

A recent study[4] into the operation of child protection registers in eight local authorities over eighteen months found six children who died during the course of the study. The death of children, either directly or indirectly resulting from parents' actions, is not acceptable to society at large or professionals in the field. However, the objective finding that child deaths happen has to be accepted. Refusal to accept the fact of child murder and child manslaughter stokes moral outrage which demands a scapegoat, be it parent or social worker, whose deficiencies can be publicly vilified so that the illusion can be preserved that we live in a society where children do not die at their parents' hands.

Child deaths are obviously the extreme cases of abuse. The incidence of different forms of abuse is not known or indeed likely to be known, bearing in mind that child abuse is a private activity with powerful disincentives to full reporting. On 31 March 1992 there were 38,600 children on child protection registers in England.[5] This is 6,700 fewer registrations than in March 1991 but it *cannot* be concluded that the figure represents a reduction in the incidence of child abuse. *Working Together*, the Department of Health Guide to Arrangements for Inter-agency Cooperation for the Protection of Children from Abuse, states (at para. 6.36) that the child protection register is 'not a register of children who have been abused but of children for whom there is an inter-agency protection plan'.[6] This guide also changed the categories for registration. So the reduction in numbers of children registered indicates no more than changes in the system for registration.

It has been suggested by American research[7] that only one in seven physically abused children is officially recorded. Surveys of the population at large to establish the actual level of abuse of children are faced with almost insurmountable methodological problems. First, parents may not answer questions relating to abuse honestly, and second, there is no consensus about what actually constitutes child abuse. Newson[8] found that over a quarter of boys were hit with straps, sticks and slippers. Presumably few of the parents would identify themselves as child abusers. Social workers would, however, want to know the frequency and context of such hitting, where the children were hit, whether injuries resulted, the impact on the parent/child relationship, and so on. Estimates of the incidence of sexual abuse also vary widely, not least because the definitions of sexual abuse include a range of actions from exposing a child to pornographic material through to the most serious crimes of sexual assault and rape.

The incidence of abuse is dependent on who defines the abuse. Many children are regularly exposed to threats and abuse, are frightened, become withdrawn and anxious, and sometimes experience significant harm to their health and development. Yet if such abuse is racism in action, it is not usually defined as child abuse, although the symptoms and consequences are often indistinguishable from abuse at the hands of parents.

In summary, we do not know the extent of the incidence of child abuse.

However, we do know that the extent of officially recorded abuse is almost certainly an underestimate and we must accept the fact that a number of children die each year at the hands of their parents.

THE PREDICTABILITY OF ABUSE

Each year SSDs receive an estimated 180,000 to 250,000 child protection referrals in England alone. From this mass of referrals, social workers must identify those children who are genuinely at risk. The report of the inquiry into the death of Liam Johnson made the following comments on the prediction of abuse:

> It was said to us before we started hearing evidence that if we could suggest ways in which families like this, who in no way stand out from hundreds of others with whom the agencies deal, could somehow be identified before the tragedy occurs it would be an enormous help. It will be clear from the pages that follow that although we suggest ways in which practice might be improved, we have been unable to suggest any infallible method of spotting potential child killers.[9]

In investigating possible child abuse, social workers must navigate a course between two unacceptable alternatives. The following diagram illustrates the dilemma.

TRUE NEGATIVES
Child not abused
Child not identified as abused

FALSE NEGATIVES
Not identified
Abused

FALSE POSITIVES
Identified
Not abused

TRUE POSITIVES
Identified
Abused

There are tens of thousands of 'true positives' each year, that is those abused children subject to child protection plans. Very little public attention is given to these children. The vast majority will not come to court but the children and their families receive practical help, social work support and counselling and many are the unsung successes of the social work profession. Public awareness of child protection is dominated, however, by the 'false positives' (some of the cases in Cleveland, Rochdale and Orkney) and the 'false negatives' (Heidi Koseda, Tyra Henry, Liam Johnson and so on). The consequences for the child of a misleading assessment, either a 'false positive' or a 'false negative', can be traumatic, enduring or possibly fatal. Some of the 'false negatives' (Maria Colwell and Jasmine Beckford, for example) appear to be etched in the collective unconscious of the social work profession, as well as, one hopes, its conscious awareness. Awareness of the dangers of failing to identify the extent of risk of abuse contributed to the over-use of removal from home as a response to suspected abuse in the investigation process. In some social work circles this has been known as 'playing safe'. The phrase implies false comfort, ignoring the emotional scars on children and families who have been drawn unnecessarily into the child protection net.

Checklists

Checklists of risk factors have been compiled to help in assessments. Checklists can be a valuable tool in systematically drawing together information which may be important to the assessment. The Report of the Inquiry into the death of Jasmine Beckford[10] was optimistic about the potential of checklists to identify children at risk more scientifically. However, the faith in checklists has been criticised by Parton[11] and others for exaggerating the extent to which abuse is predictable. Checklists tend to have an inbuilt cultural bias which reflects the views of the dominant culture about normal child-rearing practices. If checklists are seen by social workers and others as an *aide-mémoire* to facilitate the comprehensive and systematic analysis of information, it is likely that they can serve a useful purpose. Given the present state of knowledge, checklists cannot be used as if they were a formula in an arithmetic equation which will reliably give the correct result.

A study of children on child protection registers, by Packman and Randall,[12] found that it was difficult to differentiate the characteristics of the group of children who were removed from home from the group that stayed at home. 'Perceived low standards of care, concern about the child's health and development, a history of neglect or abuse ... were all significantly more likely to be associated with a decision *not* to admit (to care) than otherwise' (my emphasis). The authors concluded that the children on the register were 'in many respects indistinguishable from a larger population of deprived and troubled families where poverty and strained or fractured relationships interact to produce behaviours in parents and children that are potentially damaging and dangerous'.

This study did little to advance the search for a diagnostic tool that will reliably distinguish between those families where the risk of harm is so serious that removal of the child is necessary, from those families where the risk of harm is likely to be less than the damage that would probably be caused by the child's removal. Into this equation of balancing risks must be added what is now known empirically about the experience of children in care.

The forecasting of future abusive behaviour is perhaps even more uncertain than economic or weather forecasting, especially as judgements have to be made about the long-term welfare of the child, not just the predicted level of risk next week or next month. There are associations between child abuse and individual and family characteristics. The occurrence of previous abuse is perhaps the most significant. As Professor Stevenson[13] wrote: 'It flies in the face of common sense, for example, to suggest that a man with a long-standing history of violence to children is no more likely to do it in the future than a man with no such history.' It is relatively easy to decide the balance of risk where a man has an established pattern of abuse against a number of children over a number of years during different stages of his life cycle. Most cases are less clear-cut. What if non-accidental injury is the only reasonable explanation for a 6-month-old's broken leg, despite the parent's denial? What if there is a second similar fracture but it is against a background of excellent care?

While previous incidents of abuse are associated with the likelihood of further abuse, they are not causative or predictive. The same is true of other factors associated with child abuse – for example, a parent's experience of child abuse as a child, or the existence of a violent marital relationship. They serve mainly as *post hoc* explanations of abuse which has occurred. Social workers have to draw together all the relevant information about a family, weigh the evidence and make a professional judgement. There is no substitute for this rigorous process.

Just as the previous section ended with a reminder of the limited state of knowledge of the incidence of child abuse, so this section concludes with a warning of the very limited state of knowledge of the predictability of abuse of children.

The Context for Decisions

Social workers' judgements derive from a complex field of interacting influences. Professional training and a knowledge of research are central. This informed and objective source is mediated by two further influences shared by all: public opinion on the one hand, and personal values, experience and what can best be described as prejudice on the other. However, this section first summarises some of what is known about the effects of removing children from home into the care system and emphasises the importance of providing family support services to promote the welfare of children in need.

Effects of the Care System

There is now a body of empirical evidence which demonstrates that there are apparently persistent features of the care system that jeopardise the welfare of children. The Department of Health has published two accessible summaries of the relevant research in 1985 and in 1991.[14, 15]

Perhaps three of the most worrying effects are placement instability, disruption of education and dwindling links with families.

In a recent large study of 5,800 children experiencing over 10,000 placements, a third of placements did not last as long as planned.[16] A study of teenagers leaving care found that only half of the children who came into care before their teenage years were able to leave from a stable long-term placement.[17] During the two years' fieldwork of the Rowe study, 57 per cent of children had no moves at all but thirty-eight children had five or more moves and six of these children had not reached school age. Each move usually disrupts the child's closest relationships with adults and friends and very often necessitates a change of school. Three-quarters of the Garnett study left care with no educational qualifications, which compares with 11 per cent of the total population of school leavers from the authorities studied. This is consistent with previous information collected about the educational hazards of being in care.[18]

Children Lost in Care[19] highlighted the dwindling links between children in care and their families, and brought social workers' attention to the practical obstacles which are sometimes placed inadvertently in the way of children keeping in touch with their parents. Because of the degree of placement instability, links with families are likely to be the only stable and enduring relationships for many children and should therefore be carefully nurtured.

The extent of youth homelessness among care leavers is clearly established by research. Care leavers have been adversely affected by changes to the social security system whereby the full adult rate of benefit is not available until the age of 25 on the assumption that families will take responsibility for young adults who have to rely on benefit. Young care leavers without family support are often materially, socially, emotionally and educationally ill equipped to meet society's expectation that they become independent at 18.

Recent scandals about residential care in Staffordshire and Leicestershire have further reinforced concern about the welfare of children in the care system. Some social workers have become so despondent about the ability of the care system to help children effectively that they are leaving children at home where they receive unacceptably low standards of care. The challenge for the care system is to provide a quality of care that promotes the welfare of children and compensates them as far as possible for any disadvantage previously suffered.

Family Support Services

At the same time SSDs must work towards the achievement of the progressive objectives of the Children Act, to provide family support services for children in need and to promote their welfare while living with their families as long as this is consistent with their best interests. Previous childcare legislation only aimed to provide family support services in order to prevent reception of children into care. The Children Act objective is far broader. Bringing children into care is hazardous, yet in the past they had to come into care in order to qualify for a range of often expensive services. The Act intends that such services should be provided for the child to secure his or her future within the family so long as that is in the child's interests. This change of emphasis has not yet been fully recognised in all local authorities: 'some are being rather slow to develop adequate children in need initiatives and are finding it difficult to move from a social policing to a more proactive partnership role.'[20]

Public Opinion

There is no clear public consensus on what constitutes child abuse or the role of the state in policing intra-familial relations. The growing emphasis on children's rights as distinct individuals and the statement of the belief in the paramountcy of children's welfare inevitably means some curtailment of family autonomy. Where to draw the line between the competing value positions of children's rights and family autonomy is broadly a political decision. Within the broad framework agreed by Parliament it is a judicial decision. Within the somewhat more detailed framework of case law precedents, child protection professionals exercise their discretion. Overarching the whole process, both influencing and responding to decisions, is that amorphous yet powerful creature, public opinion.

A difficulty for practitioners is the shifting nature of the line defining the point of permissible or indeed required intervention. In the wake of well-publicised child abuse scandals in private boarding schools during the passage of the Children Bill, new powers were granted to local authorities to enter and inspect standards of welfare in such schools. Since then, the need for this extra regulatory burden has been re-examined in the light of representations from some residential schools. The Children Act gave statutory recognition to the autonomy claims of older children in respect of certain medical examinations but subsequent case law has appeared to restrict the exercise of this recently granted autonomy. Thus at both the political and judicial levels which create the legal framework for child protection activity, there is change and movement which in part reflects the changes in public mood.

Child Abuse Inquiries

Especially during the 1980s, a key opinion former on child protection matters was the series of child abuse inquiries. The phenomenon of child abuse public inquiries has been subject to interesting analysis.[21] The inquiries have usefully identified shortcomings in inter-agency practice, social work training and the law. They have also, however, played a part in engendering an atmosphere of fear inimical to the dispassionate appraisal of risk which is central to child protection work. Child abuse inquiries also became a rather macabre form of public entertainment, somewhat akin to the televising of criminal trials in the United States. They have emphasised the depravity and pathology of individuals and the personal mistakes of the professionals involved, at the expense of an analysis of the social context of child abuse. *Child Abuse: A Study of Inquiry Reports 1980–1989*[22] ends with an awareness of the limits of the inquiries. That the 1990s have not so far been dominated to the same extent by media coverage of child abuse inquiries should be a step towards a more dispassionate background for child protection work.

Inquiries and their media coverage played their part in the development of defensive social work, which confuses the protection of the child with the protection of the social worker's professional standing and the SSD's public reputation.

The Professional's Values, Principles and Prejudice

Social workers have to evaluate the significance and meaning of information collected regarding a child thought to be at risk. As I have argued earlier in this chapter, it is unusual for the information to point unequivocally to a definite course of action. The social worker must assess the information and this process presents wide and sometimes dangerous scope for the intrusion of unchecked personal values and prejudice.

A dominant philosophy or set of attitudes about child abuse tends to emerge in a particular area office or SSD which tends to hold sway at different times. Such a dominant philosophy is often collectively held and is reflected in local authority and area child protection committee policy statements. Its influence may extend to the local magistracy. It has value in ensuring that social workers are practising within an agreed framework and thus provides some safeguards against idiosyncratic behaviour by individuals. However, the dominant philosophy brings attendant risks and cannot be a substitute for carefully weighing the evidence in each individual assessment. Dominant philosophies are sometimes reactive to cases which have gone tragically wrong; they may derive from an institutional defensiveness following a public outcry in one authority, or they may be influenced by articulate adherents of a certain school of thought such as that advocated by the NSPCC in Rochdale.[23] Compared to other professionals working in child protection, social workers tend to have lower status, less professional training and often lower educational attainment. It may therefore be difficult for them to resist or question the dominant philosophy. Resisting the dominant philosophy leads the individual worker towards a position of isolation, high stress and possible professional suicide. Where there is a dominant philosophy and a strong culture of group decision-making (for example, in planning meetings or child protection conferences), the individual social worker may defer to this group process and accept what amounts to an invitation to abdicate personal and professional responsibility. Yet the individual social worker is often the only person in a position to observe, collect and analyse all the evidence regarding a particular child and family.

Because of status differentials and often insufficient training, social workers do not always manage child protection conferences properly. The conference is too frequently the forum for inter-agency rivalries and inter-professional power struggles[24] where personal judgements and impressions are shared without challenge, rather than a forum for scrutinising information and relating the information gathered to the action to be taken in each individual case.

The summary of recent childcare research[25] concludes (p. 77) with a persuasive plea for social workers to pay more attention 'to the whole question of evidence – how to gather, test, record and weigh it'. The word 'evidence' does not here have the legal meaning of documents relating to a court hearing, but the wider sense of 'facts which lead to conclusions which must be at the heart of every decision'. This question is of central importance throughout the research studies. The alternative to a rigorous approach to the weighing of evidence is to rely on personal impressions, current trends, dominant philosophies and generalisations.

Social work training will have to pay more attention to the development of critical thinking; that is the ability to suspend judgement until all the relevant facts are known. This is the opposite to gaining an impression based on prior assumptions and then looking for information to substantiate the initial impression.

'Assumptions', 'mental sets', 'values' and 'beliefs' are words that social workers use to describe their own attitudes rather than the harsher and arguably more accurate word 'prejudice'. The failure to develop the facility of critical thinking in child protection work gives unacceptable scope for the application of unfounded assumptions and biased impressions. Because of the enormous powers that social workers hold over families involved in the child protection process, a willingness to challenge such assumptions is essential if the criticism of authoritarian prejudice is to be fairly rebuffed.

Social workers and others working in the child protection field must re-examine their assumptions, beliefs and understanding of their knowledge base in the light of the first two years' court data since the implementation of the Children Act. It is time to construct and test hypotheses about the meaning of the approximately 50 per cent reduction in court proceedings regarding child protection. The attractive and reassuring explanation that the Children Act 'cured' much child abuse is amusing but implausible. A second explanation suggests that there are now thousands of children at risk of abuse being left without court protection because the threshold criteria for care in s. 31 are too high and social workers are relying inappropriately on working in partnership with parents. This seems a possible explanation and requires further study. Third, the impetus, training and legal requirements of the new Act, coupled with the exposure of social work decision-making to a more specialised, trained and often higher level of court adjudicators, compel social workers to scrutinise more rigorously their evidence of the need to remove children. Social workers and allied professionals in the child protection field must address the question of why they felt it necessary to remove compulsorily over three times as many children from their families in 1990/1 as in 1991/2.

I suggest that an overestimation of what we know about abuse and the predictability of abuse, as well as underdeveloped critical analysis of the evidence, have played an important part. The overestimation of knowledge and the underdevelopment of critical analysis in a field as emotionally charged as child protection provide dangerous and inviting opportunities for the influence of personal prejudice.

REFERENCES

The views expressed in this chapter are those of the writer and not of the Department of Health.

1. J. Gibbons *et al.*, *Operation of Child Protection Registers*, (forthcoming).
2. B. Corby, *Working with Child Abuse: Social Work Practice and the Child Abuse System* (Milton Keynes, Open University Press, 1987).
3. PAIN (Parents Against Injustice), *Child Abuse Investigations: The Families' Perspective* (1992).
4. *Op. cit.* (n. 1).
5. *Ibid.*
6. Department of Health, *Working Together under the Children Act 1989* (London, HMSO, 1991).
7. E. Birchall, in O. Stevenson, *Child Abuse: Professional Practice and Public Policy* (Hemel Hempstead, Harvester Wheatsheaf, 1989).
8. J. Newson, *Seven Years Old in the Home Environment* (Harmondsworth, Penguin, 1978).
9. London Borough of Islington, *Liam Johnson Review: Report of Panel of Inquiry* (1989).
10. London Borough of Brent, *A Child in Trust: Report of the Panel of Inquiry Investigating the Circumstances Surrounding the Death of Jasmine Beckford* (1985).
11. N. Parton, *Governing the Family: Child Care, Child Protection and the State* (Macmillan, 1991).
12. J. Packman and J. Randall, 'Decisions about Children at Risk', in P. Sills (ed.), *Child Abuse: Challenges for Policy and Practice* (1989), pp. 90 and 108.
13. O. Stevenson, *Child Abuse and Public Policy* (Hemel Hempstead, Harvester Wheatsheaf, 1989), p. 165.
14. Department of Health, *Patterns and Outcomes in Child Placement* (London, HMSO, 1991).
15. Department of Health and Social Security, *Social Work Decisions in Child Care: Recent Findings and their Implications* (London, HMSO, 1985).
16. J. Rowe, M. Hundleby and L. Garnett, *Child Care Now: A Survey of Placement Patterns* (BAAF, 1989).
17. L. Garnett, *Leaving Care and After* (National Children's Bureau, 1992).
18. S. Jackson, *The Education of Children in Care* (University of Bristol, 1987).
19. S. Milham, R. Bullock, K. Hosie and M. Haak, *Children Lost in Care* (Gower, 1986).
20. Department of Health, *The Children Act Report 1992* (London, HMSO, 1993).
21. *Op. cit.* (n. 13).
22. Department of Health, *Child Abuse: A Study of Inquiry Reports 1980–1989* (London, HMSO, 1991).
23. P. Dale, M. Davies, T. Morrison and J. Waters, *Dangerous Families: Assessment and Treatment of Child Abuse* (Tavistock, 1986).
24. Bridge Child Care Consultancy, *Sukina: An Evaluation Report of the Circumstances leading to her Death* (1991).
25. *Op. cit.* (n. 15).

10

The NSPCC in the 1990s

Barbara Joel-Esam
Solicitor, NSPCC

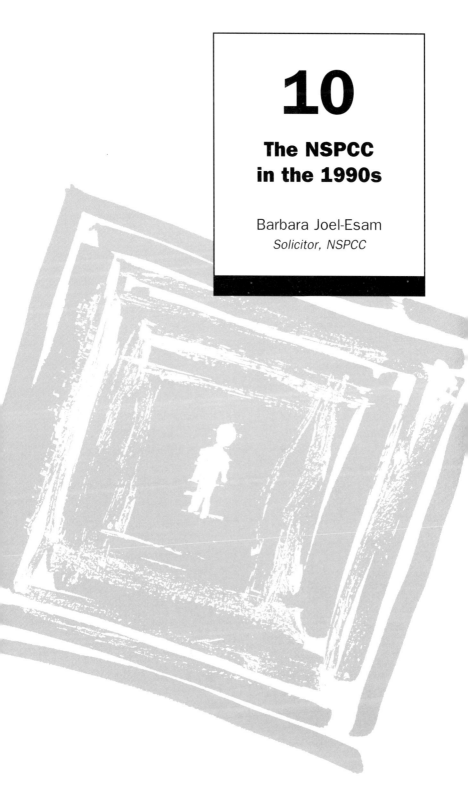

The National Society for the Prevention of Cruelty to Children (NSPCC) is in a unique position among voluntary and statutory organisations in that it focuses exclusively on abused children and families where abuse has occurred and on the prevention of child abuse. For many, the NSPCC conjures up an image of the uniformed inspector, or 'cruelty man', out and about in the neighbourhood carrying out investigations into the physical abuse of children from 'deprived families'. The NSPCC has undergone many changes since the era when such a description was at all accurate and has evolved to develop a wide range of strategies to help children and their families.

BEGINNINGS

To understand the role of the NSPCC in the 1990s, it is helpful to look at its beginnings. The NSPCC started with the formation of the London Society for the Prevention of Cruelty to Children in 1884. The Society was founded at a meeting held at Mansion House on 8 July and the Revd Benjamin Waugh was appointed Honorary Secretary. He virtually shaped the Society during its early years. The first office and shelter was opened in October 1884 at Harpur Street, Bloomsbury, in London and three years later the first 'aid committee' opened in Bristol (aid committees were later reorganised into branches and districts). There was no legislation to protect children (although legislation in the form of the Prevention of Cruelty and Improper Treatment of Cattle Act 1822 existed to prevent cruelty to animals!). Children then faced the same problem that women faced until relatively recently in relation to domestic violence and rape in marriage. Since child abuse was seen as taking place in domestic situations, the protection of children was considered to be out of the sphere of appropriate Parliamentary intervention. The Society was, however, able to bring cases of cruelty to the attention of the police and the courts with allegations of criminal assault. Even then, most children's cases could not be heard because evidence had to be given on oath and the nature of the oath had to be understood. The NSPCC secured an amendment to the criminal law in 1885 so that a child's evidence could be received without oath where the truth of what the child was saying could otherwise be proved. The Society operated shelters to which children could be sent by the magistrates pending a decision in their case. There were many destitute children who were also housed in the shelters.

By 1889, after five years of campaigning, the Prevention of Cruelty, and Protection of, Children Act 1889 was finally passed. It became known as the 'Children's Charter'. The legislation allowed under certain circumstances a legal transference of parental control; it enabled the police to obtain a warrant to enter a home where there was reasonable cause to suspect that a child was in danger; the police were given powers of arrest in relation to anyone ill-treating a child; children would no longer be left to beg in the streets as it became illegal to cause or procure a child to be in any street for the purpose of begging; and further restrictions were established to regulate the employment of children. In the same year, the chief commissioners of the Metropolitan and London police issued instructions that all cases of cruelty to children reported to them should be handed to the Society to be dealt with. The Society adopted a new name on 14 May 1889 – 'The National Society for the Prevention of Cruelty to Children' – which has remained unchanged to the present day.

In 1894, as a direct result of the Society's efforts, the Act was amended so that abuse through mental cruelty was recognised for the first time, and failure to call a doctor to a sick child became unlawful.

AUTHORISED PERSON STATUS

In 1904, the Prevention of Cruelty to Children Act was passed and the NSPCC gained 'authorised person' status for the first time, which it retains today by virtue of the Children Act 1989. With the consent of a Justice of the Peace, the NSPCC could remove abused children from their home without police assistance. Uniformed inspectors, initially known as the 'children's men', were employed. This nickname evolved so that the inspectors became known colloquially as the 'cruelty men'.

With the creation of the welfare state following the Beveridge Report in the post-war years, the NSPCC had to reconsider its role. In 1960 the NSPCC agreed to consult with case coordinating committees of the local authorities before taking legal action on cases. In 1969, inspectors stopped wearing uniforms as part of a policy to change the NSPCC's image and practice. At the end of 1974, non-accidental injury registers were established nationally, following guidance from the Department of Health and Social Security. The NSPCC Special Units were responsible for managing the registers in their areas.

In the early 1970s there was a gradual move towards professional qualification for all inspectors and this was accelerated following the much-publicised child death of Maria Colwell in 1973. However, the lack of speed in moving towards universal professionalisation resulted in the NSPCC being somewhat marginalised during this period. The process of moving towards the employment of qualified staff only was nearly complete by the mid-1980s when a child death occurred in a case in which the NSPCC was involved – that of Heidi Koseda. This event triggered the final acceleration to complete the process of professionalisation.

In the early 1980s the NSPCC developed a new vision of its work with children. A centenary charter restated the Society's commitment to the protection of abused children and the prevention of child abuse, and went on to pledge to set up a nation-wide network of sixty child protection teams. The charter aimed to combine the best traditions of the inspectorate with the innovative work of the Special Units. A mix of staff from both backgrounds came together to form the new child protection teams. There was a further commitment in the centenary charter to developing NSPCC's training and professional education activities in line with the tradition of its pioneering role.

THE 1990s

Perhaps the most significant feature of the NSPCC today, arising from its strategy for the 1990s, is that it provides direct services to children and families which reflect the specific needs of the local community. Management has been devolved into eight regions, each of which has responsibility for deciding how to respond to the needs of the children in its area. The implementation of the Children Act 1989, just over 100 years since the first legislation was passed to prevent child abuse and protect children, has helped to focus the development of the NSPCC's preventative strategy and services for children at risk of significant harm. The NSPCC is researching the impact of the 1989 Act, and indeed the Criminal Justice Act 1991, with a view to seeking further reform in the legal system for the benefit of children.

Today the NSPCC is dependent on public donations for nearly 90 per cent of its income. This financial framework nurtures the independent status of the NSPCC, which empowers the Society to be innovative and radical as a challenging voice to change society's approach to children and to promote the welfare of children both regionally and nationally.

REGIONAL SERVICES

The NSPCC strategy for the 1990s is to bring services closer to children and families. Over eighty-five child protection teams and projects have now been established across the country and these are incorporated into the eight regions. The process of setting up the teams and projects has been based on negotiations with local professional networks. The teams are no longer required to conform to the previous uniform rigid structure of five social workers with one team manager. Some teams have staff seconded from social services departments. They no longer provide a standard range of services. The staffing levels, the scale of projects and the life-span of projects all vary. The devolution of decision-making power and responsibility to the eight regions has radically affected the provision of regional services. Each of the regions is charged with the task of assessing the nature and level of local need with a view to providing services for children and families which are tailored to suit those local needs. Clearly this work cannot be done in isolation and co-operative contacts and partnerships with statutory and voluntary organisations have been, and continue to be, forged. All of the teams and projects work closely with local professionals to develop their expertise in particular aspects of child protection work.

In Cornwall there is a project that looks at the way in which communities respond to child abuse, and formulates strategies for prevention. The South East London Child Protection Team has developed particular skills and expertise in conducting investigations and joint interviews with the police under the *Memorandum of Good Practice for Interviewing Children*, despite all the attendant problems. The child protection team in Surrey is developing a child witness support programme which will be provided with the help of volunteers.

Investigations are seen as part of the core services that should generally be provided by the local authority. The NSPCC will, however, become involved in investigations in specialist situations. Some teams, for example, have developed services in conjunction with local authorities to investigate cases where children have been abused in care, or cases of out-of-home abuse and organised abuse. The NSPCC's independent authorised status is crucial in these cases.

Increasingly teams and projects carry out assessment and treatment programmes, taking referrals from local authorities. In Manchester there is an NSPCC child sex abuse consultancy service which deals with sex abuse cases and provides consultancy and training as a specialist resource across the nation. A Leicester Helpline was set up to provide advice and counselling to victims of institutional abuse in a case which attracted national interest. The project was run by the NSPCC but at the request of the local authority. A similar service has now been established in North Wales. The London region of the NSPCC is involved in a joint project with Centrepoint to set up the first refuge for children at risk (under s. 51 of the Children Act). This will be an integrated project combining the child protection skills of the NSPCC workers with Centrepoint's expertise in providing services to homeless young people.

OFFENDERS

There is a growing number of teams and projects doing work with offenders, as it is increasingly recognised that this work is an important part of protection for children. An NSPCC project in Oldham is working in conjunction with the probation service to provide group work for sex offenders. A joint project with the probation service, the NSPCC and other agencies in Craigavon, Northern Ireland, offers a programme of several weeks' duration for young offenders with a focus on analysing the reasons for abuse and working to break behaviour patterns that lead to abuse. In Tyne and Wear a project is working with young perpetrators of sexual abuse through a group-work programme.

EVALUATION

Evaluation is a vital element in the work of the teams and projects, and a number are participating in a research study, funded by the Department of Health, in evaluating the treatment programmes. There is also a recognition of the importance of working with parents and children to evaluate how they have felt about the services they received from the NSPCC and the local authority. The NSPCC is involved in a joint project with Cardiff University which looks specifically at children's experience of service provision.

EQUAL OPPORTUNITIES

There are a number of initiatives across the regions which are working to translate the NSPCC's commitment to equal opportunities into action. There is a national project for assessing the level of service provision to black children and families which aims to improve practice. This is a joint project being conducted by the NSPCC and the Race Equality Unit at the National Institute for Social Work. In addition, this joint initiative is linking with other NSPCC projects across the organisation which are concerned with services to black children. This is with a view to developing an overview of service provision in all regions in order to encourage the sharing of information about some of the lessons learned. The following are examples of such projects in the regions:

- Black Families Project, Nottingham (Eastern Region). This project is based on research into the service needs of black communities and will be specifically for a defined inner city area of Nottingham. The project will provide a drop-in centre, group work, counselling and advocacy to both parents and children.

- The South Asian Community Project (Wales and West Midlands Region). This is a two-year project, working in conjunction with Warwick University, which focuses on the needs of South Asian families for child protection services in the Sandwell and Coventry areas. It will involve service providers and policy makers in reviewing their services to meet the specific needs of children and families from these communities.

- Bristol Child Protection Centre (South West Region). This is a proposed project which would link with area health trusts to pilot a scheme to develop services to Asian women who have been sexually abused as children. Work has already begun on extending contacts with black workers and community groups with a view to reviewing and evaluating care services to ensure that all work addresses discriminatory practice.

- Ealing Project (London Region). There is an education project planned which will be based in primary schools in the borough. The pilot project would be in a school where a significant number of pupils, parents and governors are of Asian origin. There is also a possibility of placing a child protection worker with an Asian GP who has expressed concern at the under-reporting of child abuse among her patient group.

- Black Youth Counselling Service, Manchester (North West Region). This is a young black people's counselling and advice service in inner Manchester, aimed at young people who are suffering from or at risk of abuse, including racial abuse. This project is based on the work of the Manchester Black and In-Care Group.

NATIONAL VOICE

The NSPCC, through its Public Policy Department, provides a national voice for children. Campaigning for reforms in favour of the needs and rights of children is one of the primary functions of the Public Policy Department which is located at the national headquarters. The strategy for the 1990s led to the appointment of a lawyer, a UK Parliamentary officer and a European officer to join an existing team made up of policy development officers, researchers, trainers, information officers and communications officers.

POLICY DEVELOPMENT

As part of the NSPCC's Strategy for the 1990s, the Policy Development Group is committed to providing a challenging voice to change society's approach to children and promote the welfare of children. This is accomplished through public education campaigns such as the 'Act Now for Children' campaign, which used advertising and leaflets and focused on how to cope with the effects of stress on family life. Public education campaigns have been a primary tool used by the NSPCC in its efforts to assist the prevention of child abuse. In recent years, the NSPCC has emphasised the association between child abuse and such material stress factors as unemployment and debt, which may contribute to parents going 'over the top' and harming their children. This is a real sea-change for the NSPCC as previously it followed a policy of simply not dealing with these issues. This change in policy is now seen as essential in order to protect children. The NSPCC has also adopted a clear stance against corporal punishment and the Society is an active member of EPOCH (End Physical Punishment of Children).

With the aim of keeping child abuse at the forefront of politicians' minds, there is a running programme of lobbying Members of

Parliament, including the suggestion of possible Parliamentary questions to be asked of ministers by members of both Houses of Parliament. A European strategy has been developed to ensure that children's rights and needs are on the agenda for the European Parliament and Commission.

With a view to promoting the continuing development of quality professional child protection practice, submissions are made to inquiries, for example in relation to organised abuse and out-of-home abuse. An ongoing evaluation of the practical effects of legislation on children is a further important area of work for this group. This includes a threefold analysis of the strengths and weaknesses of the legislation *per se*, the success of the court system in implementing the legislation and the way in which social workers and other professionals have developed their practices to accommodate the legislation. The basic question at the root of the threefold analysis is whether the legislation is as effective as it can be to meet the needs and rights of children. The effects of the Children Act 1989 on children and the position of child witnesses and victims within the criminal justice system are examples of issues at the heart of this work.

RESEARCH

Policy development is dependent on research for the continuous gathering of information on children's needs, the causes of child abuse and services to protect children. Major research studies carried out by the Society have included a two-year project to interview adults with disabilities who experienced child abuse as children, a study of the investigation of child sexual abuse from the child's perspective, and an analysis of the characteristics of over 26,000 children placed on child protection registers over an eighteen-year period. The Research Group has also conducted an evaluation of the pilot of the Home Office *Memorandum of Good Practice for Interviewing Children.*

The Headley Library at the NSPCC headquarters was established in 1974 and now holds the largest multi-media collection of child abuse/protection literature in the United Kingdom, with more than 20,000 items. It is available to external users as well as NSPCC staff. The library can carry out literature searches of its database to provide reading lists on any area of child abuse/protection. Information briefings are produced, summarising the current state of knowledge on child protection issues.

CHILD PROTECTION TRAINING

The NSPCC provides a range of training and consultancy services through its Child Protection Training Group and through a number of local teams across the country. The group organises an annual training programme consisting of short courses, seminars and conferences, based primarily at the purpose-built NSPCC Training Centre at Leicester. The annual programme is designed for internal staff and for other professionals from different agencies and disciplines. It draws heavily on the practice experience of NSPCC operational staff. One of the programmes that has been particularly successful is 'Training for Trainers', which helps trainers to develop their knowledge and expertise. It is linked to National Vocational Qualifications and Post-Qualifying/Advanced Award Standards.

The Child Protection Training Group is also responsible for developing a number of training packs, videos and materials for use by trainers and by child protection staff. A Child Protection Training Resource Unit has recently been opened at Leicester, which provides a reference service to those involved in child protection training; access to training materials and to advice and consultancy from trainers and from an audio-visual technician is available. The consultancy advice includes help with identifying training needs and with planning, designing, delivering and evaluating the effectiveness of training. The group is also active in influencing the development of national child protection training and advocating for those involved in this work to have access to high quality learning opportunities linked to accreditation.

CHILD PROTECTION HELPLINE

The NSPCC Child Protection Helpline was developed as a result of a three-year project covering Greater London. The success of this initiative persuaded the NSPCC to launch the National Child Protection Helpline in March 1991. The Helpline provides a national child protection service through a free 24-hour telephone line in England, Wales and Northern Ireland. It is provided for anyone concerned about, involved in or at risk of child abuse, and also offers advice, counselling and information to callers.

The Helpline receives and assesses incoming child protection enquiries and passes all items that are considered to require a further response to the appropriate statutory agency (the social services department or the police), or to an NSPCC child protection team or project. Calls are received from the general public, parents, children, relatives and professionals. The Helpline has made it easier to reach and talk to professional staff at the NSPCC.

The Helpline currently employs sixty telephone counsellors who are professionally qualified (virtually all hold Certificates of Qualification in Social Work) and have extensive individual experience in the field of child protection work. (The freephone number of the NSPCC Child Protection Helpline is 0800 800 500.)

THE WAY FORWARD

In some ways it is a heartening time for the advancement of children's rights. For the most part the Children Act 1989 is a very progressive and positive piece of legislation. However, the untimely nature of its implementation – in the midst of a recession with ever-increasing levels of poverty – threatens the hopes raised by the legislation. The vast resource implications of meeting the requirements of 'children in need', of establishing a sufficient number of family centres and of providing proper support to children and their families mean that practice is falling far short of the ideals now enunciated in child protection law. Sadly, this is at a time when resources are frequently severely overstretched. The provision in s. 17 of the Children Act is a duty, not just a power, to safeguard and promote the welfare of children in need; but there are enormous difficulties in monitoring the proper discharge of this statutory duty and hard-pressed local authorities are in many cases forced to provide only for those at high risk of significant harm. The challenges relating to prevention, assessment and treatment of child abuse must be met at least in part by the voluntary sector acting both alone and in partnership with the statutory sector.

Much remains to be done for child witnesses and victims in criminal proceedings where the court procedures put many children through intolerable experiences. Social workers complain that the welfare of children is being sacrificed in favour of the process of obtaining 'good evidence' for the prosecution of the alleged abuser. Children complain that their experience of court was as bad as the abuse itself.

The problems centre on a failure to recognise that children are vulnerable because of their young age. They must be allowed to tell their story at their own pace, not in a one-off interview lasting under an hour, as the *Memorandum of Good Practice* suggests. They must be allowed to give all of their evidence, including cross-examination, at an early stage. This would ensure that they would be able to remember their evidence and would also enable them to begin to put the experience of abuse behind them. Instead they are made to tolerate the long delays, averaging around ten months, before these cases come to trial. They should be allowed to receive therapy where appropriate, and not made to wait for therapy until the trial is over in order to counter accusations that their evidence has been contaminated. Defence barristers must be required to use language that children can understand and must adopt a manner which is appropriate for a vulnerable witness. Children are not equipped to cope with badgering and aggressive, leading questions.

The NSPCC is promoting new legislation (which has already been implemented in Scotland) whereby children can give their evidence on commission. This would mean that both examination-in-chief and cross-examination would be recorded on video prior to the trial. It would go a long way towards alleviating the present problems of delay. The evidence would be received by a commissioner who would either be the trial judge or a lawyer appointed by the judge. Prosecuting and defence lawyers would be present.

The NSPCC is committed to the continuing development of creative and potent strategies for challenging society's approach to children, and to keeping the issue of child protection high on the agenda of all those with power to make decisions that affect children.

11

The Official Solicitor in Child Abuse Cases

Michael Hinchliffe

Senior Solicitor,
Official Solicitor's Office

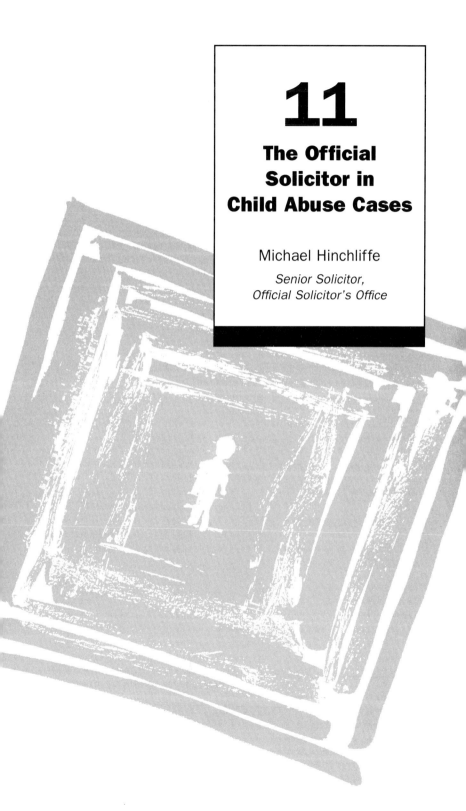

From October 1991 to October 1992 I sweated along with the rest of the Official Solicitor's children staff over the interpretation of the transitional provisions of the Children Act 1989. Many of us thought that the department's work would be drastically cut back when public law wardship cases finally went the way of the dinosaurs. Now, however, the office is handling the same number of cases as before, although there is an increasing number of private law cases.

The office of the Official Solicitor to the Supreme Court has its origins in the Middle Ages and has always been concerned with the representation of those unable to defend their legal rights, such as children, the mentally ill and prisoners.

The present office of the Official Solicitor to the Supreme Court is created by s. 90 of the Supreme Court Act 1981, and is a full-time public office. The Official Solicitor, who is appointed by the Lord Chancellor, must be a solicitor or barrister of ten years' standing and holds office on terms similar to a judge. The office is staffed by 115 full-time and a small number of part-time civil servants, of whom 40 are engaged in children work. These are organised into five divisions of case workers, each managed by an experienced senior executive officer under the supervision of a lawyer.

FUNCTIONS

The functions of the Official Solicitor are many and various. His role in child abuse cases is a particularly important one.

In Children Act proceedings and wardship the Official Solicitor may represent a minor or mentally disordered parent. In the majority of cases, he acts for the child himself. When representing the child who is the subject of proceedings, the Official Solicitor always acts as solicitor as well as guardian ad litem. The role of the office in Children Act and wardship proceedings is described in more detail below.

THE OFFICIAL SOLICITOR AND CHILDREN

What follows is a detailed description of the Official Solicitor's activities, particularly as they relate to cases involving allegations of child abuse.

Appointment

In proceedings under the Children Act and in other family proceedings, the Official Solicitor may be appointed to act for the child in exceptional circumstances. In public law proceedings (specified proceedings as defined in s. 41 of the Children Act 1989 and rule 4.2 of the Family Proceedings Rules 1991) he may act for the child only in the High Court and if the child does not have a guardian ad litem from the panel. In private law proceedings (non-specified proceedings) the Official Solicitor may act in either the High Court or the county courts, but it is more usual for the child's interests to be protected by the appointment of a court welfare officer (Lord Chancellor's Direction of 7th October, 1991 [1991] 2 FLR 471, and Court Business Practice Note, Family Law, February 1993).

The Official Solicitor only rarely appoints a panel guardian ad litem to act as his agent – for instance, where he or she has already been involved in the case and has established a particular rapport with the child. In private law proceedings there is no provision for funding panel guardians ad litem and so only the Official Solicitor or a suitable private individual may act as the child's guardian ad litem.

A Typical Case

A typical children case would begin with the court file being sent to the Official Solicitor's office. Although the bulk of the work on a particular case would normally be handled by an individual case worker, each case will be reviewed by the divisional manager or the supervising lawyer on a regular basis and referred where necessary to the Official Solicitor himself who devotes a good deal of his time to children work. In addition, there is a deliberate pooling of knowledge of individual cases to ensure continuity of representation, should the primary case worker have to relinquish the case for any reason. The work is essentially a corporate effort.

Having read the court file, the case worker will interview all individuals (quite apart from the strict parties to the proceedings) who may have a view that is relevant to the child's welfare. Advice will be given on the joinder of third parties as appropriate in accordance with Family Proceedings Rules (FPR) 1991, r. 4.11(6). The evidence is reviewed and where necessary supplemented by the Official Solicitor's own expert evidence. In child abuse cases the Official Solicitor commonly instructs child psychiatrists, paediatricians or other medical experts who may in particularly difficult cases spend many hours interviewing the child and other individuals involved. Although the case worker will of course see the child in every case, he or she will, in cases where an expert is asked to carry out interviews, deliberately keep his or her own interviews to a minimum for the sake of the child. Reports may be commissioned from school teachers, police and, occasionally, other professionals involved in the case.

The Official Solicitor will ensure, so far as it lies within his power to do so, that statements and reports are filed promptly and that the hearings of children's cases in which he is involved are not subject to unwarranted delay. Because the Official Solicitor does not apply for legal aid in children's cases, work on a case can be started as soon as he accepts the appointment as the child's guardian ad litem.

Although prepared by the individual case worker, the Official Solicitor's report is always reviewed and signed by the Official Solicitor himself or his deputy.

The Hearing

The Official Solicitor briefs counsel and (through his representative) attends the main hearing with counsel. He is thus able on behalf of the child to cross-examine witnesses as well as tender his own witnesses and make submissions. If, exceptionally, the Official Solicitor has not had time to prepare a formal report, then his representative will be prepared to undergo cross-examination.

Specific tasks may be imposed upon the Official Solicitor by the court either before or after the main hearing – for instance, the determination of details of contact ordered by the court. Cases under the Children Act, and therefore the role of the guardian ad litem in them, are generally finite and end with the determination by the court of the application. On the other hand, it is still common for wardship cases to remain live in the Official Solicitor's office indefinitely. There will be periodic referrals to court, sometimes at very short notice. One of the family lawyers on the Official Solicitor's staff is always available to deal with any complicated or urgent matters which may require his attention. The Official Solicitor will also deal with any other proceedings or legal problems with which the child may become involved and, if appropriate, he will initiate applications on behalf of the child.

In the performance of his duties, the Official Solicitor 'is much more than a mere guardian ad litem. He is at once amicus curiae, independent solicitor acting for the children, investigator, adviser and sometimes supervisor' (*Re G* [1982] 1 WLR 438 at 442).

There has been no change in the overall number of children cases in the Official Solicitor's office since the Children Act came into force. However, the proportions of public law cases and wardships have declined. In 1990, 30.9 per cent of his cases were private wardships and 46.3 per cent were public wardships. In 1992, only 19.8 per cent of his cases were wardships and 21.9 per cent were specified proceedings.

Voice of the Child

The Official Solicitor sees his primary function as being to give the child a voice in the proceedings. The child is always seen by his representative, whatever the child's age. The Official Solicitor's submissions are based on his assessment of the best interests of the child, having due regard to the child's wishes according to his or her age and level of understanding.

It must be acknowledged that there may be occasions when the views of the child are so fundamentally inconsistent with what the Official Solicitor perceives to be in his or her best interests that the Official Solicitor feels obliged to make an alternative submission to the court. An example is the infatuated teenager who wishes to continue an association with a known paedophile. This is sadly not an uncommon situation. The views of the child in such circumstances have, of course, always been presented in the Official Solicitor's report and at the hearing the child is given an opportunity to present his or her views to the judge in private.

Older children now, of course, have the right to instruct a solicitor in all Children Act and wardship proceedings. In public law cases this is achieved by decoupling the child from the guardian ad litem, and in private law cases by removing the guardian ad litem (r. 9.2A, FPR 1991). It is unfortunate that the rules are not flexible enough in private law cases to allow the guardian ad litem to continue to assist the court after the child has been granted leave to instruct his or her own solicitors. As far as the Official Solicitor is concerned, he will always advise older or more able children of their right to seek separate representation, even if there is no apparent difference of opinion. When granting leave to the child in public law cases to instruct his or her own solicitor, the court may give directions as to the future duties of the guardian ad litem and may give leave for the guardian ad litem to have his or her own legal representation (r. 4.11(3)(b), FPR 1991). This is likely to be a formality in the case of the Official Solicitor since he always acts as his own solicitor in such cases.

Examination and Treatment of Children

Before any psychiatric or other medical examination or assessment of a child can be carried out for the purpose of children proceedings, the leave of the court must be obtained. The sanction for failure to obtain leave is that no material obtained from such an examination or assessment may be used in evidence without the leave of the court (r. 4.18, FPR 1991). This applies to most Children Act proceedings, including applications for care or supervision orders, child assessment and emergency protection orders, as well as s. 8 orders. The position is essentially the same in relation to wardship and matrimonial proceedings by virtue of the Practice Direction of 21 February 1985. It is also worth noting the Practice Direction of 15 October 1987, which provides that leave of the court is required to disclose documentation in wardship proceedings to any non-parties, including medical experts. In fact s. 12(1) of the Administration of Justice Act 1960 prohibits unauthorised disclosure of any evidence or information relating to any children proceedings. Care must always be taken that leave for disclosure has been obtained before passing information to experts even by way of preliminary consultation. The Lord Chancellor's Department is currently conducting a review of access to and reporting of children proceedings (Consultation Paper dated August 1993).

Particularly with younger children who may not be competent to refuse assessment or treatment themselves, there may be instances when it is felt necessary to seek to protect them from premature or otherwise inappropriate attention in a child abuse investigation. The correct procedure would be to apply for a prohibited steps order. The onus would then be on those seeking to carry out further investigations to apply to court for the order to be lifted. This approach was confirmed recently by the Court of Appeal in the case of *D* v. *D* [1993] 2 FLR 804, when it was held that the county court had no inherent jurisdiction to make such orders vetoing assessment or treatment and that even the High Court could only do so in wholly exceptional circumstances.

It is very important in all of this to remember that the mature child (the child of 'sufficient age and understanding') is given the statutory right to refuse to undergo a medical assessment in the context of applications for child assessment orders, emergency protection orders or care or supervision orders. There are further provisions in the Children Act, in schedule 3, in which the mature child is given the right to refuse to be examined or treated pursuant to supervision orders. There is, perhaps surprisingly, no equivalent right of veto for the child in relation to specific issue or prohibited steps orders. The then Master of the Rolls, Lord Donaldson, acknowledged this inconsistency in the case of *Re W* [1992] 3 WLR 758, at page 770E. In that case, the Court of Appeal overruled the objections of a 16-year-old anorexic girl to specialist treatment by exercising the inherent jurisdiction. Douglas Brown J more recently adopted the same approach in *South Glamorgan County Council* v. *W & B* [1993] 1 FLR 574. In each case, the child was in the care of the local authority and so the court was barred from making a specific issue order or a prohibited steps order. Such orders under the inherent jurisdiction overriding the views of a competent minor in relation to treatment (and, by implication, assessment) will only be made in exceptional circumstances. Those investigating suspected child abuse should always, therefore, before proceeding to arrange examination or assessment, ascertain and as far as possible accommodate the views of the child. Early legal advice should be taken in cases of doubt.

The Lessons of Cleveland

One type of case which has been designated (Lord Chancellor's Direction dated 7 October 1991) as particularly appropriate for the involvement of the Official Solicitor is what might be termed the 'spider's web' case. Typically, an individual or group of people is under investigation by the police for alleged child sexual abuse and at the same time the local authority institutes child protection measures which lead to civil proceedings in relation to a number of children in one family or a group of families. The Official Solicitor represented the children in a number of such cases before the Children Act 1989 came into force, notably the 'A' case (reported as *Re A and others (Minors) (Child Abuse: Guidelines)* [1992] 1 FLR 439) and the Rochdale case (*Rochdale Borough Council* v. *A and others* [1991] 2 FLR 192). We were able to see at first hand the failure to follow the recommendations of the Cleveland Report and to hear the criticisms made by very experienced High Court judges of local authority and police practice. Common complaints included the fielding of untrained interviewers and the lack of an overview of the case for the local authority. Whether these issues have been sufficiently addressed throughout England and Wales remains to be seen.

Such cases where civil and criminal proceedings overlap do, however, present fundamental difficulties for practitioners. If charges have been brought but the civil proceedings cannot wait for the outcome of the criminal proceedings, what is the guardian ad litem to do? If the guardian ad litem commences enquiries, he or she (or his or her expert) may be called on to give evidence at trial and runs the risk of prejudicing the criminal case. If the guardian ad litem waits, he or she may be failing in his or her duty to the child. The Official Solicitor has therefore decided that in such cases, he must issue a summons for directions in the civil proceedings. In the first case in which this was done, the judge ruled that the Official Solicitor's representative was to visit the children at that stage only to introduce herself and our expert was to produce a paper report (without interviewing) which was not to be disclosed to those involved in the criminal proceedings.

Release of Evidence

The Official Solicitor is also often asked to consent to the release of evidence from the civil to the criminal proceedings. This also presents a problem in the balancing of relevance against prejudice to the child since the trial judge is best placed to assess relevance but the civil judge is best placed to assess prejudice. The answer at present seems to be to invite the applicant (usually the defendant in the criminal proceedings) initially to seek leave in the civil proceedings for the documents in question to be released to the defendant's legal advisers only. An inter partes summons can then be issued with an affidavit in support, specifying what is sought. If there are objections to disclosure which cannot be met by release of documents with blanked-out sections, the matter must be referred to the trial judge with the suggestion that he or she may wish to call on the services of the Official Solicitor as *amicus curiae* to help on the issue of prejudice. I have recently appeared in this way with counsel at a trial at the Old Bailey.

COSTS

The Official Solicitor is under a duty as a public servant to seek to cover his costs wherever possible. Where parties are privately funded, as is the case commonly with adoptions, he will seek an undertaking as to his costs at the outset of the case. In public law Children Act cases he will seek an undertaking from the local authority as to at least a proportion of his costs. In order to avoid protracted argument in individual cases, agreements have been reached with a number of local authorities fixing a percentage of the Official Solicitor's costs which will be met by the local authority in each of its cases in which he is involved. The Official Solicitor does apply for legal aid in some categories of cases, for instance those in which he acts for a minor or mentally disordered parent. It has always been his policy not to apply for legal aid when acting for the child subject in family proceedings. If necessary – for instance, in cases where there is no local authority involved and all parties are legally aided – the Official Solicitor's costs will be met from central government funds.

CONTACTING THE OFFICIAL SOLICITOR

The Official Solicitor's office is at 81 Chancery Lane, London WC2A 1DD (tel. 071-911 7127). Members of staff are always available to try to assist with queries. More specifically, since the Children Act 1989 came into force, the Official Solicitor has operated a telephone helpline for panel administrators and guardians ad litem.

It is worth emphasising that the Official Solicitor covers the whole of England and Wales and his officers conduct interviews and cover hearings wherever and whenever necessary. Currently there are over 6,000 live cases within the office.

12

Child Abuse: a Police Perspective

Susan Hall
*Detective Inspector,
Northumbria Police*

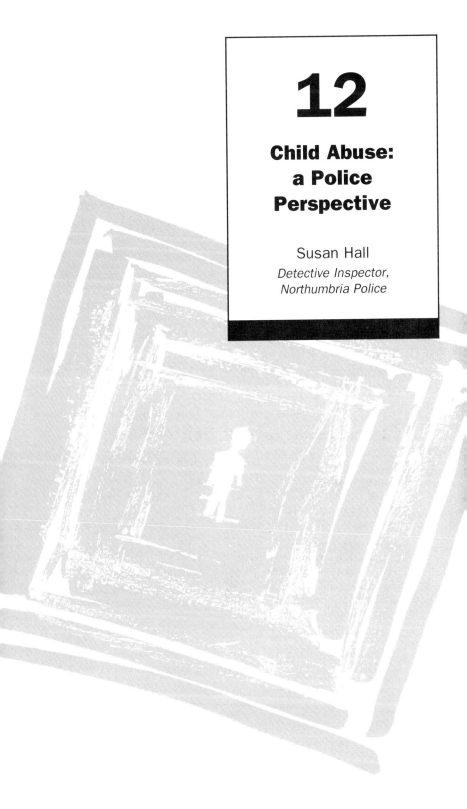

For many centuries people believed that it was necessary to beat good into children, and to punish them physically when they did wrong. Until 1889 even Parliament appeared unconcerned with the way in which parents treated their children, regarding the most barbarous cruelty as beyond public intervention, since children were still not regarded as citizens in their own right. It was not until the National Society for the Prevention of Cruelty to Children and others campaigned against such cruelty that the Prevention of Cruelty to, and Protection of, Children Act 1889, popularly known as the 'Children's Charter', was passed. This gave magistrates the power to issue a warrant to permit the entering of a home if there was suspicion of ill-treatment; it gave the police the power to arrest those suspected of ill-treatment; and it gave the courts the power to remove such children from their parents. This Act was later consolidated and extended by the Children Act 1908 and the Children and Young Persons Acts of 1932 and 1933. There have since been a number of Acts, all aimed at protecting children. Fortunately, children are now recognised in law as having rights. The Children Act 1989 has created a legal framework for the care, protection and upbringing of children and the provision of services to them and their families.

The underlying principle of the Act is that the welfare of the child is of paramount importance. Over the years, society has continually been made aware of the prevalence of child abuse. The Colwell inquiry, for example, in 1973 highlighted the issue as a major social problem requiring state intervention. This and subsequent inquiries served to highlight the failings within the child protection system. This, in turn, has led to many changes as workers within the field have continued to develop their strategies.

The purpose of this chapter is to outline the role of the police in the current child protection system and to demonstrate how they have responded to recent changes in legislation and recommended practices. Because of the complexity of this work, it would be impossible to examine their role in isolation. I have therefore concentrated on the inter-organisational and inter-professional relationships that exist between the police and the other agencies within the multi-agency system (health, social services, education, etc.).

THE POLICE: THE DUTY TO INVESTIGATE

The role of the police is the protection of life and property, the prevention of crime, the detection of crime and the apprehension of offenders. Under the Children Act 1989 we have a duty to investigate all cases of suspected child abuse. It is our duty to establish whether a criminal offence has been committed, to identify the person(s) responsible and to institute criminal proceedings where appropriate. The welfare of the child remains our primary concern throughout.

The decision of whether or not criminal proceedings should be instigated rests with us. However, it is then the responsibility of the Crown Prosecution Service to review and, where appropriate, conduct proceedings on our behalf. The decision to prosecute will normally depend on three factors: whether there is enough evidence to prosecute, whether it is in the public interest and whether it is in the interests of the child.

Over the years our role in such cases has been the cause of much concern. This concern centres on two issues: firstly, the appropriateness of a police investigation, and secondly, the appropriateness of a prosecution. Many feel that police intervention is unnecessary. This dilemma is a clear illustration of the wider debate concerning the balance and tension between justice and welfare, and between punishment, retribution and rehabilitation in the penal system. There are some who are ambivalent about the value of punishment: intellectually they feel that punishment is ineffective as a treatment, but because they have been brought up to expect punishment to follow wrongdoing, they feel uneasy when this does not happen. To the police officer, child abuse is a crime; to the social worker it is a social problem. The social worker's understanding of behaviour is a causal one and his or her approach may be one of removing those causative factors. Thus, if the abuser is treated like a criminal, how can the worker establish the trusting relationship which will enable help to be provided?

Dilemmas such as these must be formally addressed. It is therefore imperative for individuals to work closely together and to have a clear understanding of each other's roles and responsibilities. If we are to succeed in providing an effective child protection system, there must be trust and respect between the different agencies.

No Prosecution

It is not unusual in child abuse cases for the police or the Crown Prosecution Service to decide against criminal proceedings. The evidential requirement of the criminal court is proof beyond reasonable doubt that the defendant committed the offence, with the burden of proof resting with the prosecution. It may be decided that proceedings should not be instigated due to a lack of evidence.

Similarly, such a decision may be made on the grounds that criminal proceedings would not be in the interests of the child. There is growing concern that child witnesses are being exposed to unnecessary suffering at the hands of our legal system. There are some who would argue that the ordeal of a police investigation, followed by months of waiting, culminating in the actual court appearance, actually constitutes further abuse for the child. Involvement in a criminal investigation and trial clearly causes considerable stress for the child(ren) and is bound to have some effect. Just how much permanent damage it causes is much less clear. It is therefore important for us to reach a balance, avoiding unnecessary stress and suffering while ensuring the protection of the child(ren) from further abuse. Unfortunately there may be occasions when the detrimental effect of a child being interviewed and subsequently called to court will be outweighed by the greater public interest of protecting society. All of the facts must be considered in every case.

Although the final decision to institute criminal proceedings rests with the police, we will always endeavour to seek the joint agreement of all agencies involved. The decision to prosecute is a serious one and is never taken lightly.

NORTHUMBRIA POLICE

In recent years Northumbria Police has become more actively involved in the field of child protection. In 1985, for example, police child protection units were introduced. The Force now has six such units, staffed by highly trained officers (each unit consists of one detective sergeant and several constables) who work closely with social workers. Northumbria Police also benefits from an excellent women doctors' scheme. This was established in 1983 and provides an excellent service for all victims of sexual abuse. Initially the scheme was aimed at adult victims, but it expanded with the recruitment of paediatric staff to cope with the growing number of young victims. The doctors provide a 24-hour call-out system, seven days a week. Over the years they have gained a considerable amount of expertise in this field, and regularly take part in joint training programmes with our officers. All medicals take place at specified locations, which are either at local hospitals or at purpose-built suites. The aim is to reduce the trauma of the medical examination.

In 1992 a Detective Chief Inspector was appointed Child Protection Unit Coordinator for the Force. He provides a central liaison point, not only for the Force's six child protection units, but also for the six local authority child protection officers. He currently sits on a Procedures Working Party, alongside his counterparts from the local authority, the NSPCC and the Crown Prosecution Service. They are currently involved in drawing up procedures, systems and guidelines for the implementation of the *Memorandum of Good Practice* issued by the Home Office and the Department of Health.

A training subgroup has also been formed, and it has recently produced a programme for joint training. It is currently working on an investigative action pack and a memorandum of good practice.

The Detective Chief Inspector also provides continuity for the six area child protection committees (ACPCs), having the rare privilege of sitting on all of them.

The Force has seen the emergence of eight new video-recording suites.

These have been developed in conjunction with the ACPCs and are located throughout the Force.

The Force is continually developing its strategies for dealing with child abuse and lays great emphasis on the need for inter-agency collaboration. There is thus close liaison with all agencies concerned and in particular with the social services departments which investigate all cases of suspected abuse with us.

The responsibility for the investigation of suspected child abuse within Northumbria Police Force is vested in the Chief Superintendent, CID. He nominates a representative of the Chief Constable to sit on the ACPCs within the Force area. This is normally the Detective Chief Inspector who also has responsibility for the management of the divisional child protection unit. The unit investigates all allegations of suspected intra- or extra-familial abuse (see Appendix 1, p. 192) and those cases of stranger abuse which are identified as being more appropriate for inter-agency investigation (after consultation with the Child Protection Unit Sergeant or senior CID officer responsible for the unit). As indicated, all investigations are carried out jointly by the police and social services.

A Multi-agency Approach

It is well established that child protection work requires good inter-agency cooperation. Indeed, it has been government policy since the publication of the Colwell Inquiry in 1974. Northumbria Police recognises the importance of working closely with other professionals and regards inter-disciplinary work as an essential process in the task of attempting to protect children from abuse. Excellent relations have been developed over the years between the police, the social services, health and education departments and voluntary organisations. Workers from these agencies are now benefiting from working and training together, and a mutual understanding of each other's roles has resulted. One needs to be very conscious of the fact that these agencies have very varied structures, as well as different powers, duties, objectives, work styles and value systems. They must be able to combine their skills if an effective child protection system is to be achieved.

Butler-Sloss LJ in the Cleveland Report (Cm 412, London, HMSO, 1988) highlighted the importance of a good working relationship and the need for close liaison at all times. This was reinforced in the Children Act 1989 which provided a legal framework for a multidisciplinary approach.

One must not underestimate the effect that an investigation has on a family. Public confidence in our child protection system will only be attained if a proper balance is struck. Northumbria Police continue to strive to achieve such a balance.

THE INVESTIGATION

The purpose of the investigation is to discover whether the child is, or is likely to be, at risk of harm and thus in need of protection. Throughout the investigation the child's welfare remains our prime consideration. Because of this, the entire investigative process has to be well thought out and must follow a structured plan. There must be clearly defined policies and procedures for all concerned.

Communication with the child's parent(s) and/or those with parental responsibility is considered at all stages and although the presumption is for parents to be fully involved, there may be circumstances where this is considered inappropriate (see Appendix 2, p. 193).

The process begins with a referral of concern about a child. This can come from one of a number of sources and is passed to either ourselves or to social services. After liaising with each other, routine checks are made with the other agencies involved with the child – for example, the health visitor, general practitioner, teacher, etc. – and all information is collated.

A strategy meeting follows (with all relevant professionals present) where the nature of the referral is considered and all available information examined. It is at this stage that a decision is made as to whether or not an investigation is appropriate. If this is so, the situation is assessed and any necessary decisions made (for example, for an urgent medical examination and/or for removal of the child from the home). The investigative team is established and a structured plan of action drawn up.

THE INTERVIEW

The next stage is for the investigative team to prepare and plan for the interview. This interview will invariably be video-recorded. Before the interview takes place the team will consider a number of factors, for example:

- the child's state of mind

- the child's physical condition

- the child's age

- the intelligence of the child

- the time and venue of the interview

- who should be present at the interview

- who should take the lead in the interview.

One must remember that the purpose of the interview is to discover what, if anything, has happened. The interviewer must therefore approach the interview with an open mind.

As already stated, the majority of interviews are video-recorded. Under the provisions of the Criminal Justice Act 1991, such a video recording may be admissible in the crown or youth court as evidence-in-chief. The child will not be allowed to be examined in chief if all of the relevant matters have been covered in the interview. The video recording of the interview is therefore the first stage of the child's evidence and the questions put to the child by the police officer and/or social worker replace the examination of an advocate in open court. The Act does, however, give the court power to reject the whole or part of the video on the grounds that, 'in the interests of justice', it ought not to be admitted. It is therefore vital that the interviewer is aware of the rules and the law on interviewing children.

The quality of the interview will depend largely on the skills of the interviewer. Conducting an interview with a child victim must be one of the most demanding interview situations and requires careful preparation. It is important for the interviewer to listen and to allow the child to control the flow of information.

Conducted correctly, the interview has many advantages. It provides a clear record of the child's own account, showing his or her demeanour at the time of the interview. The tape can be used in a subsequent trial as evidence-in-chief; it may precipitate an admission if shown to a suspect, or a guilty plea if shown to an accused; and it can be used in civil proceedings, either before or after the criminal proceedings.

Once the interview is over, the team will always conclude by reassuring the child. The child is never left wondering what is going to happen next and will always be given a contact telephone number (alternatively, this may be given to the parent or guardian).

The team will evaluate the information available and plan further action. A case conference will be called (if appropriate) and all those who can provide information about the child and the family will be invited to attend. The conference provides a forum at which members share information and decide whether or not the child has been abused and/or whether or not the child is at risk of abuse in the future. An action plan will be drawn up, clearly defining individuals' roles and responsibilities. A decision will also be made as to whether the child's name is to go on the Child Protection Register.

In short, the case conference formalises the decision-making process, giving it added status and significance in relation to other case decisions.

TRAINING

Child protection work is extremely complex and it is, therefore, vital for workers to have the necessary skills, knowledge and expertise. This means regular training for all those working with children and the updating of training programmes. Much of the training is carried out jointly with social services. This ensures a common standard of training and gives workers an understanding of each other's roles.

In 1993 a new training course was introduced in the Northumbria Police area. It was designed by the training subgroup of the practice and procedures group for all those involved in the interviewing of children. The programme, which takes cognisance of the Home Office *Manual of Good Practice*, focuses on three main areas: law, practice and procedure.

1. *Law*
    (a) Legislation:
       - The Children Act 1989
       - Police and Criminal Evidence Act 1984 (PACE)
       - The Criminal Justice Act 1991
    (b) The role of the Crown Prosecution Service
    (c) The courts – youth, magistrates, crown, civil
       - court craft
       - rules of evidence
2. *Practice*
    (a) Planning and preparing
    (b) The interview
       - introduction
       - rapport
       - free narrative
       - questioning
       - post-interview: evaluation
3. *Procedure*
       The video interview
       - when to video
       - consent

- explanation
- transcripts
- persons present
- use of technical equipment
- copying and storage of tapes

Training is seen very much as a continuing process, with the course providing only the basis for a much wider training programme. Individuals are constantly learning and gaining experience. They are encouraged to develop their own individual skills and are helped in overcoming weaknesses which may have been identified. They are regularly updated on changes in the law and on recommended procedures.

CONCLUSION

Although we have undoubtedly made great progress in the field of child protection, there is still much work to be done. The true incidence of child abuse has never been known, and it is highly unlikely that it ever will be. What is known, however, is that our children are still in need of protection. Every day, children are at risk of abuse from those closest to them. We must accept that, given our current state of ignorance, the weaknesses of humans and the imperfect world in which we live, children will continue to be abused. We must tackle the problem head on. Emphasis must be on prevention rather than treatment. We all need to be aware of the antecedents of abuse, and concentrate on times at which children at risk may be identified.

We must also remember that detection is only the beginning: it is essential that, through case conferences, review committees and other means, we take the necessary measures to prevent further injury. We must all use our resources to the full and strive towards a well-planned interdisciplinary system. Our children rely on us: we must not let them down.

APPENDIX 1

Child Abuse: Definition in Accordance with Northumbria Police Standing Orders

Child abuse is an all-embracing term and, depending on the alleged offence, may relate to children who have not yet attained the age of 18 years.

Child abuse includes offences of physical assault, sexual offences and assaults or neglect within the following criteria:

1. All physically injured children where the nature of the injury is not consistent with the account of how it occurred or where there is definite knowledge or reasonable suspicion that the injury was inflicted, or knowingly not prevented, and includes children to whom it is suspected poisonous or other noxious substances have been administered or where a child is sexually assaulted or abused by:

    (a) Any person having custody, charge or care of the child or by another child within the immediate family (intra-familial abuse).

    (b) Any adult known to the child but not as at (a) above (extra-familial abuse).

    (c) Any adult not as at (a) or (b) above (stranger abuse).

2. Children who have been persistently or severely neglected. This may include persistent failure to provide food, hygiene, warmth and clothing.

3. Children who suffer from non-organic failure to thrive or emotional abuse where their behaviour and emotional development have been persistently and severely affected.

4. Children who are in a household with, or which is regularly visited by, a parent or another person who has abused a child or young person and are considered as a result to be at risk.

APPENDIX 2

Circumstances where the welfare of a child dictates that contact should not immediately be made with the parents

1. Where either or both of the parents are alleged or suspected to be the abuser.

2. Where risk of significant harm to the child is feared from either or both parents or where other children in the same household are felt to be at risk of significant harm.

3. Where a child of sufficient age and competence expressly wishes its parents not to be informed of the early stage of an investigation.

4. Where only one parent is alleged or suspected of an offence against its child, consideration needs to be given as to whether the other parent should be informed.

5. Where any other weighty reasons apply.

Where any of the circumstances above apply, the investigation team must discuss, record and attempt to resolve the issues.

Where a decision is made not to inform the child's parent(s) and/or others with parental responsibility, the decision must be justified and a careful record kept of the reasons. In such circumstances legal advice should be sought.

13

Interviewing Children: Psychiatric Aspects

Dr Stephen Wolkind
Consultant Child Psychiatrist

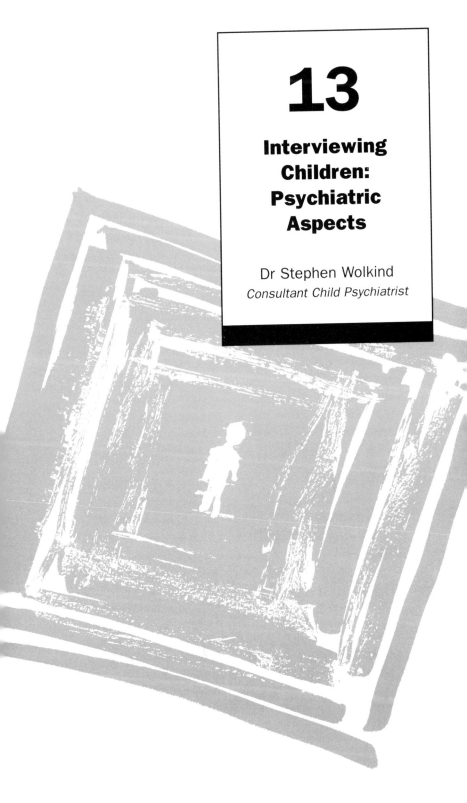

It is clearly not feasible in a brief contribution to give any form of guidance as to how one should or should not interview children, in particular those who may have been abused. An excellent account is available[1] but, of course, reading must be combined with discussion with experienced practitioners and with supervision. By looking, however, at the nature of the psychiatric techniques of interviewing and at the way in which we assess children, one is compelled to go beyond a technical exercise. Inevitably it leads to the purpose of the interview and the role of child psychiatrists in the field of abuse and to what might be expected of them when they give evidence in courts of law. I will attempt to look at the psychiatric process, at the diagnostic systems we use, at the psychiatric indicators of sexual abuse and at the way in which we use the concept of emotional abuse.

It is often assumed that a major role of the psychiatrist is to use his or her skills to determine 'the truth'. Hollywood and, on occasion, real life, have shown psychiatrists using depth or hypnotic techniques to enable a 'patient' to confess to a murder or rediscover other lost memories. Such an approach might seem ideal to help a child who is repressing unpleasant experiences or who lacks the vocabulary to describe how he or she might have been abused. It is, however, an unreal task to expect of a doctor and, as well as the problem of the validity of the techniques used, it poses real ethical dilemmas. The prime task of the child psychiatrist and the function of the psychiatric interview are, in fact, the same as the investigation carried out by any other doctor, namely to determine whether the patient has an illness or disorder. The need to determine in absolute terms how much of a child's story is fantasy and how much the absolute truth is of only secondary importance. I recently saw a depressed and miserable 7-year-old boy. He told me in great detail how his stepmother always put salt instead of sugar on his breakfast cereal. This had probably happened on one occasion but the actual reality was of far less interest to me than the fact that this child had chosen to tell me this story in a tone that seemed to mix anger and despair. By concentrating on this aspect of the child's contributions I was avoiding a very great dilemma which seems to have often bedevilled psychiatry – can you believe all that your patients tell you?

Freud during the 1880s became convinced that he had discovered the prime cause of adult neurotic illness when he found that his predominantly female patients would, with alarming predictability, describe scenes of seduction, usually performed by fathers. Later, after attempting and failing to obtain confirmatory details from other family members, he decided that these statements must have been fantasies and it was in the structure of the fantasies that lay the origins of the later illness. The debate about the relative importance of early life events in the genesis of psychiatric illness has continued over the years. With Freud's patients it is possible that some of their accounts were fantasies but that some, perhaps even the majority, had indeed been sexually abused as children. What Freud was probably correct about, however, was that at that later stage it was the telling of the story which was of more importance than what had actually happened. This attitude to an individual's account is of course in marked contrast to the expectations that others in different professions would have about their interviews. For police and, to a lesser extent, social workers, determining whether a child's story is true must be the first priority.

Over the last few years this distinction between psychiatric and other interviews had tended to become somewhat blurred. It gradually became apparent to a small number of professionals, including child psychiatrists, that sexual abuse of children was not a rare event but a common experience, particularly among those being referred to clinics with behavioural and emotional disorders. The task of determining the details of what had happened and presenting these to courts, in order to prevent a recurrence, became for these doctors a major priority. The difficulty was that many of the patients were too young, too disturbed or too developmentally delayed to give a coherent account of what had happened to them.

To deal with this situation a variety of techniques were adapted to help create investigative interviews. The word 'adapted', rather than 'developed', seems appropriate, for the techniques such as hypothetical and alternate questioning, discussed in some detail in the Cleveland Report, were not new innovations but ones well established and of accepted value in the psychiatric treatment of children and families. In this latter situation where the relationship between the patient and therapist is of major importance, the use of a hypothetical question such as 'and if you have really burnt the house down what might have happened to all the family?' could enable a child to open out about fears and angry feelings which might otherwise have been difficult or impossible to elicit. However, to use a question such as 'but if daddy *had* touched you down below, what would you have thought?', after a child had replied 'no' when being asked if she had been touched, is very different. It could be legitimate if this was part of treatment after other definite evidence has proved that the child had indeed been abused by her father. It is far more problematic if it is being used to obtain factual information when there is doubt about whether the abuse had occurred. Disagreements on this point split the profession, and child psychiatrists are probably secretly relieved that it was a paediatric rather than a psychiatric technique which suddenly became front-page news. The Cleveland Report suggests that considerable caution should be applied in the use of such approaches and equally in the use of sexually explicit dolls as a way of obtaining information. What was particularly worrying about some of the pre-Cleveland interviewing is that these special techniques with all their limitations were used with very disturbed children instead of, rather than in addition to, the full psychiatric assessment.

THE DIAGNOSTIC PROCESS

After these cautionary statements it is necessary to explore in more detail what a child psychiatrist can positively contribute to social services departments and courts which are deciding the future of a child. As described above, the prime task is to establish whether or not a psychiatric disorder is present. Following this, a number of subsidiary questions arise. If the answer is yes, what is the nature of that disorder, what impact is it having on the life of the child, is it linked to associated or developmental or learning difficulties, what might be its cause and its prognosis and what, if any, treatment is required? This emphasis on what might appear to be a very traditional medical approach might cause some surprise to lawyers and social workers who expect from a psychiatrist not a diagnosis but general advice on how a child's needs could be best met; for example, should a child be removed from the family for adoption or is rehabilitation to the parents feasible? To make a decision in such a case a court will have to weigh up a great number of social and legal factors. What the child psychiatrist can contribute, using his or her diagnostic model, is what impact any decision might have on a child's psychiatric state. Might a disorder improve after adoption? In a child with no disorder, might one develop were he or she to be removed from home? In both cases, what might be the long-term prognosis of the disorder? The amount of empirical research in developmental psychopathology and child psychiatry is now sufficient to enable child psychiatrists to give estimates of the probability of changes occurring in a child. The possible effects of a particular course of action on a child's psychiatric state will not in itself determine whether or not that course should be followed, but it can offer helpful information which should be included in the decision-making process. This approach lends itself particularly well to determining whether or not 'significant harm', as used in the Children Act, has occurred.[2]

If this diagnostic approach is followed, a major advantage is the very comprehensive assessment of the child that it involves. The diagnostic system used follows World Health Organisation criteria and is internationally recognised.

Much work has been done on the reliability and the validity of the various categories in the scheme. To make a diagnosis involves systematic interviewing of the child, the parents and usually the family together. Because children can behave totally differently in different settings, school and other relevant reports are required. The diagnosis made at the end of this process is a complex one. Sufficient information must be obtained to describe the child on five different dimensions or axes. The first is the actual psychiatric disorder. Its importance to those making decisions about children is considerable. Certain disorders such as those concerning a child's conduct are primarily environmentally caused and can be taken to represent the effects of significant harm. A child with such difficulties has a poor outlook for mature development if he or she continues in an environment which is maintaining that disorder. In a different setting the outlook could be quite different. With other conditions, such as an attention deficit disorder, improvement might not necessarily occur with a change of environment.

The next three axes cover the child's intellectual, developmental and physical status. Too often so much attention is paid to whether a child has or has not been abused that crucial questions about health and educational needs are not asked. The final axis deals with associated environmental and family factors. It is in this axis that abuse, whether physical, emotional or sexual, will be rated. These are in themselves not diagnoses but factors which might explain why a disorder commenced or failed to improve. It is worth re-emphasising that sexual abuse is not a psychiatric diagnosis but a possible cause of a psychiatric disorder. This is not a question of semantics but of very great practical importance. Sexual abuse can be followed by a great range of consequences from minor anxiety states to serious post-traumatic stress disorder, from slight stroppiness to severe and dangerous aggression. The sexual abuse *per se* is usually of less importance than the seriously disturbed relationship that it symbolises. The needs of any abused child would be better recognised from the overall psychiatric picture than from the fact that he or she has been sexually abused. It should be of concern that there has been a tendency to see sexual abuse as a homogeneous concept which requires special projects devoted to its treatment.

The needs of a sexually abused, mentally retarded child with physical failure to thrive and gross hyperactivity are quite different from those of a child with good academic abilities and high self-esteem who is understandably depressed by the betrayal of trust by a stepfather.

PSYCHIATRIC INDICATORS OF SEXUAL ABUSE

The two cases mentioned above illustrate how differently children who have been sexually abused can present to psychiatrists. They also should help us realise that in looking at any psychiatric disorder, there is only extremely rarely a single cause. In looking for causes we are guided by research which has demonstrated the way in which a variety of innate and environmental factors contribute to the final picture. Examples of an innate factor in the child could be a particular constellation of temperamental characteristics which many parents would find hard to cope with or cognitive deficits which make it hard for the child to understand the world around him or her and the social rules that govern it. Environmental factors would include continuing disharmony between parents, which can be devastating for the child, or unreal expectations by the child's school. The developments of recent years, the Cleveland inquiry and the advice of the Department of Health now confirm that to this list (which should be considered routinely in all cases by child psychiatrists) should be added sexual abuse. The DHSS *Diagnosis of Child Sexual Abuse: Guidance for Doctors*[3] emphasises the wide variety of signs and symptoms that might be caused at least in part by sexual abuse. Some, such as clear descriptions by the child, should give rise to severe suspicion; in others, such as unexplained changes in behaviour, suicidal gestures or running away, the suspicion should be mild or moderate. In any cases where there are not clear reasons that the disorder has commenced, sexual abuse must always be considered.

EMOTIONAL ABUSE

A point that causes a great deal of concern to child psychiatrists is the rather doubtful attitude of the legal profession to emotional abuse. The X-ray corroboration of a broken bone caused by a blow from a violent parent or physical signs of clear sexual abuse are almost gratefully received as clear evidence which will have a major impact on decision-making. In practice the physical traumata of abuse will in most cases heal within a relatively brief period and leave only minor scars. In contrast, the emotional abuse which accompanies these injuries or which more often is inflicted in the absence of physical damage can have profound effects on the individual for the rest of his or her life. The difficulty, however, is in defining emotional abuse and in deciding when this is sufficiently harmful to warrant legal intervention. Almost any type of parenting behaviour, such as giving too little spending money or preventing a child from sucking his or her thumb, could in theory be taken by some as evidence of emotional abuse. The need is to try to restrict this and find a set of criteria that do require intervention. Here again the psychiatric assessment can be of help.

Clearly a first point must be evidence of grossly abnormal parenting of a quality that is outside the acceptable and wide range normally seen. Examples would be a total absence of any positive affirmation of the child or sets of expectations that no child could reach. This must be accompanied, however, by the presence in the child of a psychiatric disorder which is known to be largely caused by environmental factors and which has a poor prognosis for later development. Insistence on this point can upset social workers confronted by examples of totally neglectful parenting. If the child is not showing evidence of a disorder there may be very strong social reasons for intervening but this cannot be thought of as emotional abuse. One might disapprove of particular patterns of family life but the absence of an obvious psychiatric disorder in the child should lead to very considerable caution. The third point is that, in addition to the presence of the two criteria described so far, there must be the refusal or inability of the parents to use or accept appropriate intervention. I deliberately say 'appropriate' because too often the type of intervention offered is designed to meet the needs of the therapist rather than the family. Further discussion of these different criteria have been presented elsewhere.[4]

I have ended with this brief account of emotional abuse because it brings together well the very real contribution that child psychiatric interviewing techniques can make in assessing the needs of children. It cannot be underestimated how harmful the effects of the misuse of psychiatric techniques are. Sadly, in clinical practice one is seeing children suffering from serious emotional and behavioural problems which are the result of precipitate action following on from misconceived investigations carried out by psychiatrists and psychologists. The more the child psychiatrist keeps to the traditional role of obtaining a full psychiatric history with a view to diagnosing a disorder, the more use his or her findings will be to those who have to decide the future of children.

REFERENCES

1. Jones and McQuiston, *Interviewing the Sexually Abused Child* (London, Gaskell and Royal College of Psychiatrists, 1993).
2. Adcock, White and Hollows, *Significant Harm* (London, Significant Publications, 1992).
3. DHSS, *Diagnosis of Child Sexual Abuse: Guidance for Doctors* (London, HMSO, 1988).
4. S. Wolkind, 'Emotional signs', JSWL 2, 88, 1988.

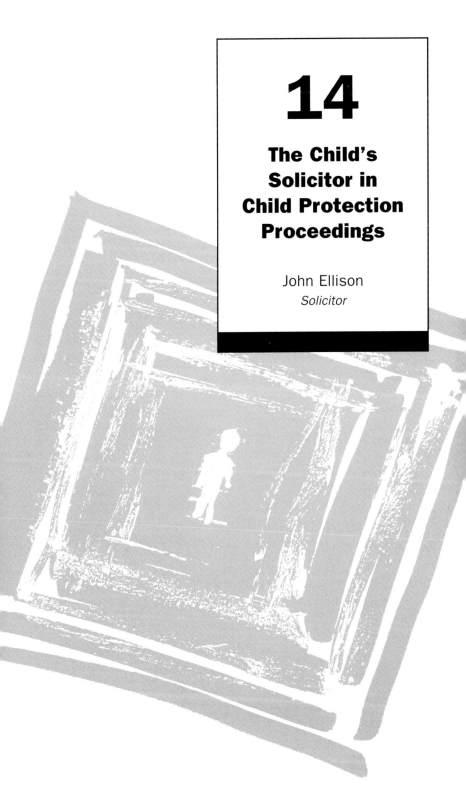

14

The Child's Solicitor in Child Protection Proceedings

John Ellison
Solicitor

Acting for the child in a care case involving a local authority is sometimes referred to by family lawyers as the saintly role. The possessor, in any given case, of the halo worn on the child's behalf, may refer to this special equipment with a touch of irony, but will still be conscious of the image of virtue and objectivity which is supposed to attach itself to the legal representation of children.

In fact, the business of acting 'for the child' is as human and vulnerable to honest error and doubtful judgement as the functions of acting for local authorities and parents.

THE PANEL

Solicitors who act for children in public law cases are expected to be limited to those who are members of the Law Society's Children Panel. Membership of the Children Panel is not achieved through extensive work in children's cases, but through the proof of slight recent experience, attendance at short courses, adequate advocacy standards and survival of a special interview. Some panel members do little work routinely in the field of care while others do a large amount.

In the public law domain, solicitors are drawn in to act for children in applications by local authorities for care and supervision orders. A solicitor for the child is also appointed when (less frequently) applications to revoke care and supervision orders are made. The appointment of a solicitor for the child in those applications is made by the guardian ad litem and, less often, by the court itself. The child may be 1 day old or 15 years (and even 16 in a few cases).

ABUSE

The nature of abuse (within the definition of which I include neglect and inadequacy of supervision) is enormously variable. A child may have been injured through physical violence (bone fractures of different kinds, burns, cuts, bruises) or, much less commonly, through ingestion of grossly inappropriate solids or liquids. A child may have been sexually abused. A child may have been left with or in the care of a fierce dog or a person no more likely than the dog to approach the standards required for registration as a childminder. A child may be at unacceptable risk of harm through poor standards of household hygiene or physical safety (animal and baby excrement, stacks of old TVs and loose electrical wires everywhere); or the unacceptable risk of harm may arise from harm (alleged or already proven) to another child in the same environment.

INITIAL PROTECTIVE ORDERS

The solicitor for the child, and the guardian ad litem who in most cases provides 'instructions', appear on the scene rather late in many cases as far as key events and decisions are concerned. Imagine this scenario: the parent has taken a young child to hospital, and medical examinations triggering consideration of protective action have taken place. Paediatricians have already considered, dithered and disagreed. A referral to social workers and police has been made. An initial police interview of a parent under arrest, possibly in the presence of a solicitor, has occurred. This process may have thrown up its own difficulties. The police interview by child protection officers may well be supported by accurate and full information and medical comment from the hospital, and may well have been thorough, fair and sensitive. It may nevertheless be none of these.

A case conference may have taken place before the local authority decision to apply for a protective order had been made and this conference may have recommended proceedings. Alternatively, the decision may have been taken by a manager within the social services department.

EMERGENCY PROTECTION

Securing a child in a safe place can be achieved through an emergency protection decision by police (of seventy-two hours' maximum duration) on the basis of information known to police through direct investigation, such as a home visit. On the other hand, a police decision could be made as a favour to a local authority unable for the moment to organise an application to a court for an emergency protection order. Professional practice by doctors, police, social workers and solicitors so far involved may have been exemplary, poor or somewhere in between.

GUARDIAN AD LITEM

When a local authority proposes an emergency protection order and the clerk to the family proceedings court to whom the application is submitted decides that the application must be heard 'on notice', the clerk may then forthwith appoint a guardian ad litem for the child. The hearing could be the next day or even later the same day, with the normal 24-hour notice requirement waived. A solicitor for the child and guardian ad litem may then, before a child has been separated from a parent, have some ability to influence events before the court's authority to allow such separation is given or refused.

A guardian ad litem allowed a few hours to become acquainted with family and professionals concerned may in practice have to rely heavily on statements submitted and oral evidence given when the application is heard. Home visits and examinations of social services records may not be practicable in the short time available before the hearing.

There is no guarantee that a guardian ad litem will be available for appointment in an emergency despite numerous telephone calls to possible appointees from the court.

WITHOUT INSTRUCTIONS

Where a solicitor acts for a young child without instructions from a guardian ad litem, and direct instructions from the child have been ruled out by reason of the child's insufficient maturity of understanding, the solicitor must represent the child 'in furtherance of the best interests of the child'.[1] This might mean in a given situation that one solicitor for the child might oppose an order whereas a different solicitor for the child might support it. Consistency of response within the profession in the same circumstances cannot be guaranteed.

EMERGENCIES

Emergencies themselves occupy a scale which runs from the obvious to the barely arguable. An obvious emergency might arise when a social worker visits a mother and finds her young child in obvious pain, unable to walk owing to a new leg injury, while the mother is not willing to explain, comfort the child or seek immediate medical attention. Such a situation might lead to police protection or to an immediate emergency protection order application. Another sort of emergency might follow the birth of a child to a mother whose two older children are both with local authority foster parents, having been first neglected and then abandoned by their mother. The case for immediate statutory protective action for the new baby may be less strong, however, than the case for immediate social work assessment of the parent's caring abilities 'in partnership with the parent' and without court applications.

The solicitor acting for a young child through a guardian ad litem gains the eyes, the ears, the experience and the judgement of an independent social work professional whose expertise must include the ability to assess the local authority social work taking place.

The purpose of the emergency protection order may be to authorise the separation of parent and child. Alternatively, the purpose of the emergency protection order may be to ensure that a child is not reunited with parents, having already been separated through admission to hospital or a stay with a non-parent. Sometimes the purpose of the emergency protection order is to prohibit removal from short-term foster parents, with whom the child had previously been placed at the parent's request. Were an order not sought, the parent with parental responsibility for the child would be able to exercise the statutory right to take the child home.

EVIDENCE

Sometimes, after examination-in-chief by the local authority solicitor of the social work witness supporting an emergency protection order, the information available to the child's solicitor and guardian ad litem remains inadequate for judgements to be made on the child's behalf. Cross-examination by the child's solicitor may be aimed at amplifying and placing in firm context the factual evidence. It may also be aimed at eliciting how far alternatives to an order have been considered, and how far, and on what grounds, it is suggested that the absence of an order will place the child at unacceptable immediate risk of 'significant harm'.

Careful cross-examination may also throw more light on the local authority plans for parental and other family contact with the child in the event that an order is made. Unsatisfactory answers to such questions have been known to flow from the absence before the hearing of adequate discussion between a social worker and a team manager, and between social worker and existing or proposed foster parents concerned. In the rush to court, questions may have been overlooked or given inadequate attention.

REMOVING THE CHILD

The question of urgent separation of child from parent is most commonly considered at hearings of emergency protection order applications, both on notice (*inter partes*) and otherwise. But the question is also sometimes considered at first hearings of care order applications, when there has been no previous police protection or emergency protection application. There will be cases when separation at the first hearing stage may be appropriate. The child's solicitor and guardian ad litem, however, may be expected to be reluctant to accept such a separation plan in many cases before investigation and assessment by the guardian ad litem have taken place, and before full hearing of the care order application.

If the parent voluntarily seeks separation from the child, it can take place with or without an order, having regard to the history and circumstances of the case. If the parent is opposed to separation, and clear grounds for an emergency protection order are absent, the guardian ad litem is likely to view an interim care order at a first hearing as premature, and the child's solicitor can expect to be instructed to oppose the disturbance of the *status quo*. The child's wishes in the matter, however, must be taken into account and such wishes in some cases have a major bearing on the position taken up on the child's behalf.

In some cases the local authority may agree to defer an application for an interim care order for a short time (a week, a fortnight or a month) until the guardian ad litem has been able to make an interim assessment. The local authority's own organisation of, and approach to, the proceedings may determine a great deal. The proceedings require an effective partnership between the social services and the legal department. Between them, witness statements must be prepared and approved, and (frequently) medical reports must be obtained.

STATEMENTS

Statements vary in quality from case to case. There is the example of a statement by a social worker which lists, sometimes in defiance of chronological order, a series of events without obvious clues as to what is intended to be ascribed importance and what is not. An entirely misleading impression may thereby be given of the maker of the statement (apparently an unselective camera, not a professional social worker working with a family). The reader at such times suspects that a local authority solicitor more comfortable with general civil litigation than children's law has masterminded the statement, oblivious to the notion that the old-fashioned but not entirely obsolete social inquiry report may be rather more helpful.

ORAL EVIDENCE

Oral professional evidence brings to the fore what is not already on paper or has been imperfectly expressed on paper. It might come out in oral evidence, for example, that the maker of a social work statement does not personally support the view attributed in the statement to the employing social services department. The personal position so brought to light may have a significant bearing on the decision to be made. Furthermore, the giver of the evidence often supplies indications of the assumptions and attitudes that underlie the professional approach adopted. These are not always of the most approved kind.

PLANNING THE COURSE OF CARE PROCEEDINGS

Vital decisions to be made by the parties in care and supervision order applications started off in the family proceedings court include the following: in which court should the application proceed; what further assessment of parenting should take place before the final hearing and over what time-scale; what additional expert assessors should be involved; how much contact should take place (where a child is not living with the parent) between the child and parent and under what conditions pending the final hearing; what further statements should be filed and what witnesses should be called. Not least to be considered is the planned time estimate for the full hearing. The time estimate must relate to the issues in dispute, the quantity of documentary material and the numbers of witnesses to be called. The child's solicitor may wish to call the guardian ad litem as a witness and possibly others too. These might be professional witnesses instructed by the guardian ad litem or associated with the local authority but not sought as witnesses by the local authority.

The complexity and volume of medical and other professional evidence may drive proceedings from the family proceedings court into the county court and then often to the High Court. Such transfer is specifically authorised by statutory instrument where proceedings 'are exceptionally grave, important or complex'.[2]

CHILDREN ACT CHANGES

At the time of writing, just two years of the Children Act in action have come and gone. The practitioner, reviewing this period, is intensely aware of changes in practical routine under the new law. Procedures feel, and are, different before the magistrates in the family proceedings court. The criminal prosecution associations of the old juvenile court have fled away. Prosecutions of juveniles no longer share a list with local authority care cases, which now stand alongside private law family proceedings.

Thanks continue to be given for the long-awaited statutory provision for parties to file statements and reports in the family proceedings court and for the statutory compulsion for magistrates to read them before the case is called on. Oral evidence is therefore now usually aimed at confirming, adding to and testing what is already on the court's file. Hearsay evidence is now admissible and respectable, if inevitably still open to charges of inaccuracy, distortion, lack of context and doubtful origin.

DELAY

The new system brings with it new delay factors. The hearing may not start because hours of reading time are required by justices. A judgment is held up because hours of consideration time (including time to formulate written findings never given in pre-Children Act care proceedings) are needed.

Within my own experience, mainly in London, advocates now take for granted sitting down throughout hearings before magistrates, often in a plain room in which advocates, parents, professional witnesses and sometimes children are elbow to elbow around a rectangle of tables. Although the atmosphere is necessarily orderly, it tends to be more informal in many courts than once was dreamt of.

In care and supervision order applications parents now benefit from legal aid provision unrelated to means and no longer need to make a case for its grant, while applications for legal aid are simple and speedy for both parents and children.

New solutions in the jurisdiction of magistrates inevitably create new dissatisfactions. While there is provision for written statements, they are not always provided; and when they are provided, they are not always within a reasonable time. Directions by the court in respect of statements and witnesses are not always regarded as seriously as they should be by the parties, local authorities not excepted. Local authorities may produce an alarming deluge of written evidence without much in the way of live witnesses to support it. There is some concern among advocates about the ability of some or most lay magistrates to judge the difficult issues often involved in hearings which may run for days.

BREAKING NEW GROUND: STARTING PROCEEDINGS ON A CHILD'S INSTRUCTIONS

Not even the Children Act allows a child, or a solicitor for a child, to apply for a care or supervision order. Only local authorities and the NSPCC can apply for such things. A child, however, has a statutory right to apply to discharge a care or supervision order.[3] Further, a child may ask a solicitor to start private law family proceedings. Exceptionally, such a course of action may be a means of self-protection for the child against a parent or other carer.

The Children Act itself does not grant a child the inherent right to apply for a s. 8 residence or contact, or other private law, order. Instead the child can, like grandparents and other relatives, apply to the court for leave to apply for such orders.

Traditionally, in private law proceedings a child has had to be represented by a friend or guardian ad litem. Under the Children Act, however, procedures are less restrictive. The 1991 rules of court in county court and High Court proceedings allow a child to instruct a solicitor directly. The child's ability to do this is supported by a new legal aid provision which allows 'green form' legal advice to be given without cost to a child with nominal or no income and capital.

Once a child has approached a solicitor, the solicitor can pursue a 'request' to the court for leave, for example, to live with or have contact with a particular person if the solicitor is satisfied, with regard to the child's understanding, that the child is able in relation to the proceedings to give instructions.[4] Alternatively the child can bypass solicitors and apply directly for permission to apply to the court.

Whether represented or not, the child will, however, only be given leave to apply for a s. 8 order if the court is satisfied that the child has 'sufficient understanding to make the proposed application'.[5] That may require 'a swift pragmatic inquiry which would involve the minimum of delay and least distress to the child'.[6] Further, a recent practice direction requires that these applications by a child for leave are reserved to the High Court.[7]

TAKING INSTRUCTIONS

A solicitor accepting instructions from a guardian ad litem is essentially an agent with an influential advisory role. On the other hand, the solicitor must cease to be an agent where he or she considers the child qualified to give instructions directly. In this context the guardian ad litem becomes the adviser and the solicitor the maker of decisions. The question the solicitor must ask is whether the child 'is able, having regard to his understanding, to give ... instructions on his own behalf'.[8]

As so often, to understand the principle is easier than to apply it. In *Re H*,[9] an academically able 15-year-old boy, S, appeared to be facing an end to his bright educational prospects as a result of emotional or psychiatric disturbance. Psychiatric assessment was sought during a care order application heard in the Bexley family proceedings court. At an early stage of proceedings, S was diagnosed to be suffering from a psychiatric disorder. Later he was thought only to be suffering from emotional disturbance. His communication capacities were not substantially impaired, for he was able to file a long statement through his solicitor and to give oral evidence. He was voluntarily present during the lengthy hearing and sat with his solicitor. By that time he was nearly 15½ years old. A care order was made, and then, S's solicitor having withdrawn, a new solicitor acting for S appealed, principally on the ground that S's previous solicitor had mismanaged his function on S's behalf. The appeal came before Thorpe J, who upheld the care order while accepting that S's former solicitor had fallen into error by accepting conflicting instructions from both S and his guardian ad litem.

Thorpe J did not accept the argument that almost any child of S's age must be taken to have enough understanding to instruct a solicitor. He acknowledged that a child of that age suffering from a mental disability or a psychiatric disorder might not have such understanding. But he was unwilling to accept that 'if a child is only suffering from some emotional disturbance then really there is little room to question his or her ability to instruct a solicitor'. He added: 'It seems to me that a child must have sufficient rationality within the understanding to instruct a solicitor. It may well be that the level of emotional disturbance is such as to remove the necessary degree of rationality that leads to coherent and consistent instruction.'[10]

All this may be excellent good sense and was supplemented by Thorpe J's further comment, which had regard to the fact that this was a case in which psychiatric evidence had been given in the family proceedings court. He said that if there was a real question as to whether the child's emotional disturbance was so intense as to destroy the capacity to give coherent and consistent instructions, there should be specific expert opinion from such experts as are already involved.[11] The child's solicitor, in such circumstances, might welcome the prospect of advice not only from the guardian ad litem but from psychiatrists appointed in the proceedings. One imagines, though, that such advice might be more welcome if originating from a psychiatrist instructed on the child's behalf rather than from psychiatrists, however apparently independent and disinterested, associated with other parties.

It is the primary responsibility of the child's solicitor by rules of court to make a personal decision. However, the Court of Appeal (admittedly in the context of private law proceedings in the county court and High Court) has ruled that the court itself is the ultimate judge of the issue.[12]

TRANSFER

Re H[13] is one of a number of reported Children Act cases which (in the view of appellate judges) should have been transferred upwards from the family proceedings court instead of being concluded there. In *Re H*, Thorpe J suggested that its special circumstances made it inherently more suitable for a Family Division judge than for lay justices. He pointed out that in the Family Division, the child could have been represented by the Official Solicitor who, in the event that the child's wishes did not correspond with the Official Solicitor's views, could remain a participant as *amicus curiae*.[14]

It was notable that none of the parties in *Re H* had urged an upward transfer, even though the time estimate for the hearing was three days. The hearing in the family proceedings court indeed ran to five days with a sixth day fixed for judgment. Thorpe J expressed the opinion that cases with a three-day time estimate were at the very boundary of the limit for care hearings to remain with lay magistrates.[15]

Where a complex case suitable for transfer upwards is not transferred, there is a risk that even if the legal representatives carry out their duties well in presenting the case, magistrates may not carry out their own task adequately in formulating their judgment. This risk is illustrated by *C v. Solihull MBC*.[16] This was an appeal by the guardian ad litem, supported by the local authority, against the making of a supervision order by a family proceedings court. The child sustained a spiral fracture of the right femur when 3 months old. The injury was caused while in parental care and diagnosed as non-accidental. There was no adequate explanation. A 2-year-old sibling, when 12 months old, had received a slap across the face from the father, causing a mark, but social workers were not concerned about the risk of repetition for this sibling. The baby had initially been placed with short-term foster parents, and then with grandparents, at an interim stage of the proceedings.

The local authority had sought a care order on the basis that a proper assessment of the parents would then be made, which would be carried out while the baby remained with the grandparents or, if the grandparents withdrew their help, with short-term foster parents. It was hoped by the local authority that, following such assessment, the child would return to the parents.

Ward J was in no doubt that a final supervision order was premature. While sanctioning the child's return to the parents, he did so on the basis of an interim residence order which was conditional upon the parents undertaking a programme of assessment and cooperating with all reasonable requests by the local authority to participate in that assessment programme. This interim residence order was linked to an interim supervision order (which was to be renewed by agreement until the assessment was completed) and the interim supervision order was itself subject to conditions for medical examination and monitoring of the child from time to time. The case was then to be further considered.

Underlying this cautious interim package of orders lay criticisms of some of the findings of facts and reasoning of the justices. It appears that instead of weighing the chances of success in the process of assessment, the magistrates gave the assessment plan no great importance. Further, the justices made no express findings as to the mother's likely cooperation, should the child be placed with and away from her and the father. Fundamentally, the child had been inadequately protected by the unconditional final supervision order made in the family proceedings court. Ward J transferred the proceedings upward with the suggestion that it should come before him for further hearing following completion of the assessment.

The lessons spelt out in the appeal judgment by Ward J constitute useful advice for both magistrates and lawyers in this glass house of legal work concerning the protection of children.

REFERENCES

1. Rule 12: The Family Proceedings Courts (Children Act 1989), Rules 1991: SI 1991/1395.
2. Article 7(1), Children (Allocation of Proceedings) Order 1991: SI 1991/1677.

3. Section 39(1), Children Act 1989.
4. Rule 9.2A(1)(b).
5. Section 10(8), Children Act 1989.
6. *Re T* [1993], *The Times*, 10 May, *per* Waite LJ.
7. Practice Direction (Applications by Children: Leave) [1993] 1 WLR 313.
8. Rule 12(1) (a), Family Proceedings Courts (Children Act 1989), Rules 1991.
9. *Re H* [1993] 1 FLR 440.
10. *Ibid.*, p. 449 F–H.
11. *Ibid.*
12. *Op. cit.* (n. 6).
13. *Op. cit.* (n. 9).
14. *Ibid.*, p. 446B.
15. *Ibid.*
16. C v. *Solihull MBC* [1993] 1 FLR 290.

15

Children with Disabilities and Special Needs: Current Issues Regarding Child Protection

Philippa Russell
Director,
Council for Disabled Children

> Yet still the myths persist that disabled children are not vulnerable – that while others may pity them they will not find them attractive or desirable, that if the children don't understand what is happening to their bodies, it can't be so harmful, that they don't feel things in the same way as others; that they cannot benefit from therapy; a series of further misconceptions that contribute to the 'let's sort out the normal children first' attitude which still, unfortunately, persists.[1]

There are about 360,000 children with disabilities (aged 16 years and under) in the United Kingdom.[2] These children form about 3 per cent of the child population in this country and many present major challenges both to their families and to statutory and voluntary services which provide support. All but around 5,500 live in a family home. The Office of Population and Census Surveys (OPCS) studies of the lives of disabled people in the United Kingdom confirmed the findings of a range of studies about the lives of families with a disabled child. Few of the families knew of the full range of services which might have helped them. Despite the then imminent implementation of the Children Act, only 12 per cent had a regular social worker and most relied heavily on child health and education services for information and advice. Only 4 per cent of families received respite care, although 50 per cent felt that their or their other children's health was adversely affected by limited opportunities to go out or to give time equally to all family members. Of those children living in residential care, 15 per cent were known to have been abused; 33 per cent had health or behaviour problems which had been impossible to cope with by the natural or foster families with whom they were living. A further 33 per cent had homes or family circumstances that were 'unsuitable' – and where the children concerned were presumably at risk.

The past decade has seen greater public (and professional) awareness of disability, with increasingly positive images about the capacity, as well as incapacity, of disabled people to make decisions about their own lives and to contribute to the planning and development of support services. Positive images are insufficient, however, without a corresponding awareness of the increased vulnerability of disabled children and their families to abuse within a variety of settings. There is also the need for improved training opportunities for all professionals working in child protection services to ensure that they are aware of disability issues and, in particular, that they know how and where to locate expert advice when required.

DISABILITY AND ABUSE: EVIDENCE FROM RESEARCH

Evidence of the possible incidence of abuse of children with disabilities or special needs currently comes mainly from studies in the United States. Sullivan, McCay and Scanlon[3] found that out of 150 children with hearing impairments attending residential schools, 75 reported sexual abuse, 19 reported incest at home and 3 reported physical and sexual abuse. Margaret Kennedy,[4] in a UK study of deaf children, found 192 suspected and 86 confirmed instances of physical and emotional abuse, with 70 suspected cases of sexual abuse and 50 confirmed. She concluded that not only were disabled children more likely to be candidates for physical or sexual abuse, but that they were likely to be abused for longer periods of time than their non-disabled peers.

From 1977 to 1983, the Seattle (USA) Rape Relief and Sexual Assault Center[5] found over 700 reported cases of sexual abuse involving children and adults with learning disabilities from the Seattle area. There was, however, considered to be significant under-reporting of the true incidence. Sexual abuse was defined in this study as rape, attempted rape or incest. Of the reported victims 99 per cent were sexually abused by relatives or care-givers.

In another UK study of sixty-five adults with learning disabilities, all attending a work activity centre, Hard and Plumb[6] found that 83 per cent of the women and 32 per cent of the men had been sexually abused. Abuse in this context was described as sexual contact caused by force, coercion or manipulation or otherwise entered into unwillingly or unknowingly. It included oral, anal or vaginal intercourse and touching breasts and genitalia.

As in the Seattle study, the researchers found that in 99 per cent of cases, the abuse was carried out by someone known to the individual concerned. Sixty-four per cent of the women said that they told someone about the abuse, but 55 per cent of them were not believed and no action followed; 60 per cent of the men were not believed in similar circumstances.

Westcott[7] has reviewed over twenty articles on the physical, emotional and sexual abuse of children with a range of disabilities. She notes that much of the current literature focuses upon *sexual* abuse (although children's vulnerability to sexual abuse may be greatly increased by emotional and physical abuse). She also notes that there has been little attention paid to the views and experiences of disabled people themselves, particularly with regard to *prevention* and *how* children and young adults might have been supported in disclosing abuse at an earlier stage. Communication between carers and disabled children and the need to listen carefully to children's fears or complaints are particularly important.

The existing literature on this subject clearly demonstrates the need for much greater vigilance in order to protect children and young people with disabilities and special needs and to ensure that these special needs are neither marginalised nor misunderstood within local child protection strategies. It also provides some important messages about the myths which need to be dispelled in order to ensure that children with special needs do not experience a double jeopardy through misunderstandings and complacency about the quality of care and life experiences which are offered to them.

Parents with disabled children often receive support from a range of sources. Respite care is one obvious popular service, although currently only around 4 per cent of parents receive it. The use of services such as respite care which remove a child from the family home may, however, in turn create problems and expose children to risk of abuse. Many parents express great anxiety about their child's safety and care. Hubert,[8] in a study of respite care for young adults with multiple disabilities or challenging behaviour, found many parents desperately anxious about the quality of care available to their child. One mother described how her son always seemed to have been heavily sedated during his stay. Another worried over her son's poor physical care, sitting in a wheelchair wet and dirty – 'so lacking in any dignity'. A third mother told how she prayed that her son would not die while he was away. Her husband felt that they must have a break and she felt that respite care was the choice that would keep the marriage together. Parents are frequently well aware of the risk of abuse.

Assessing risk for children with such complex disabilities will never be easy. Ruth Marchant[9] demonstrates the possibility of using the observations and skills of parents, staff and whatever communication aids the children use to assess the occurrence of abuse and to identify potentially abusive behaviour early and avoid it if possible. Parents themselves can be supported and encouraged to join local parents or support groups which in turn act as information givers, counsellors and advocates in getting appropriate services.

DEFINING ABUSE IN THE CONTEXT OF DISABILITY

Physical, sexual and emotional abuse and neglect are all frequently inter-linked. In the context of disability it is worth reconsidering working definitions of abuse and, in particular, looking at where they may overlap. Investment in tighter assessment procedures is unlikely to be effective unless all participants fully understand the 'add on' factors related to disability. For disabled children, therefore, working definitions of abuse may include the following:

- *Emotional abuse.* Ridicule and rejection; humiliation (for example, over problems relating to lack of self-care skills); withdrawal from favoured activities such as leisure interests or activities with non-disabled children; inappropriate patterns of care, such as lack of privacy for intimate care or bullying and teasing.

- *Sexual abuse.* Children with disabilities may be exposed to the full range of risks experienced by all children. Viewing or contributing to the production of pornographic photographs and videos, displays of sexual parts and witnessing sexual activities are aspects of non-contact abuse. Children with disabilities may not only find it harder to remove themselves from such passive activities, but also their limited social experience may not immediately indicate the inappropriateness of the activities in question. Unlike other children, many children with disabilities may require personal care which involves undressing and physical assistance from another person. Furthermore, intimate contact (including access to a child in various stages of undress) may be considered quite appropriate by other family members or professionals. Because of poor personal and sex education, many children may not only be unaware of the sexually explicit nature of some contacts, but may also lack the necessary vocabulary to communicate what has happened.

- *Physical abuse.* May also include non-contact abuse such as threats of punishment or restraint. Contact abuse may range from actual bodily harm, such as slapping or shaking, through to force-feeding; physical restraint, such as tying up or chaining, and deprivation of heat, clothing, food or medication often for the theoretical management of behaviour difficulty. Misuse of medication, often in combination with extreme exclusion diets or force-feeding have been cited in several recent court cases. They may occur in institutional settings, such as residential schools, as well as in private homes.

- *Neglect as abuse.* Many children with disabilities are smaller than their contemporaries; some disabilities are associated with developmental delays or with physical disabilities that may affect a child's appearance and lead to assumptions about younger chronological age than is actually the case. Lack of awareness of the need to treat children with disabilities in an age-appropriate way can lead to multiple problems. Any surveillance of a child with a disability should ensure that the child has received the full range of developmental checks, that any outpatient appointments relating to the child's condition have been checked and that the child's diet and general care are checked.

- *Munchausen Syndrome by Proxy – symptom abuse.* The trial of Beverly Allitt for the murder and attempted murder of a number of children in a children's ward in Humberside has highlighted a rare but regularly recurrent form of abuse, where parents, relatives or professional carers abuse, and sometimes kill, children by creating symptoms of serious illness or disability. (See Professor Meadow's observations, Chapter 7.)

- *Treatment as abuse.* The past decade has seen the escalation of a range of treatments and intervention for the care of children with disabilities and challenging behaviour. Many of these approaches are controversial and Professor Christina Lyon[10] has stressed the importance of measuring such controversial approaches which may involve medication, physical control and behavioural programmes, against the child's overall health and development. Professor Lyon concludes that 'it would be foolish to say that there will not be circumstances when those caring for children with complex needs may well be exposing the child to suffering or the likelihood of suffering significant harm'. She cites the *Children Act Guidance and Regulations*,[11] which states that, when considering a court order for any child with a disability, all agencies (whether within or without the local authority) must have a clear view about the appropriateness of any treatment for a particular child. Such considered assessment, however, may be problematic for some of the most disturbed or vulnerable children. Many of these children will be in residential settings far from their local communities. As the Castle Hill School Report[12] into abuse at a residential special school noted, 'a significant feature of our investigation was the disbelief of other professionals and their inability to accept or comprehend the extent of the abuse'. The inquiry concluded that in looking at abuse within settings purporting to provide treatment of any kind, 'an open mind and a preparedness to accept and objectively analyse improbable and sometimes unbelievable scenarios are essential'.

- *Systems abuse.* This has been more widely documented in the United
  States and Canada and reflects growing awareness that people with
  disabilities may be directly abused, or made more at risk of abuse,
  because of the organisation of service systems which fail to take
  account of the special needs of disabled people. Clearly children
  living away from home will be at particular risk of such abuse. As
  No More Victims notes:

  > Institutional life creates an ideal backdrop for abuse. Isolation and
  > emotional deprivation make people who are institutionalised more vulner-
  > able to abuse. While living in the community does not guarantee that
  > people will be protected from abuse, the improvement of the quality of life
  > and greater opportunity for the development of healthy social relations
  > may lessen the likelihood of abuse.[13]

Some 'systems' may fail disabled children because of complacency
about their safety and over-confidence in goodwill rather than training and supervision for staff. Multiple service providers can cause
fragmentation in care, with little attention being given to the actual
wishes and feelings of children.

A special factor in systems abuse may relate to the lack of independent visitors (families, friends or appointees of the placing authority)
to make certain that the child is well and happy and that there are no
problems. The Castle Hill School inquiry[14] found that the powerful
personality and perceived credibility of the head teacher persuaded
parents and professionals alike to disbelieve complaints from the
young people initially. Because many lived several hundreds of miles
from the school, informal visits by friends or families were unlikely.
Equally, within an institutional setting, abuse may become a collective activity with other pupils in turn seducing or abusing other children who may be too frightened to complain. Such an abusive environment will be particularly damaging to young people whose own
life experiences and self-esteem are very limited and who may have
no coping strategies in order to 'whistle blow'. The Gulbenkian
Report, *One Scandal Too Many,*[15] has strongly recommended that
all disabled children living away from home should have access to
independent visitors, because of their limited access to other complaints or representation procedures.

MESSAGES FOR THE FUTURE

In conclusion, the Children Act 1989 has provided us with a legal framework within which children with disabilities can be seen as 'children first'. The principle of integration and inclusion, however, should not be allowed to conceal the fact that many disabled children need considerable support in order to lead lives which are as normal as possible. It is particularly easy to see a disability as separate to the child. If we see the person, our approach to child protection and disability will become more effective.

REFERENCES

1. M. Kennedy, *Child Abuse and Disability: The UK Perspective*, Report of the Sussex BAPSCAN Conference 1992 (Chailey Heritage, 1993).
2. Office of Population and Census Surveys, *Report 3: Prevalence of Disability amongst Children*; *Report 5: Financial Circumstances of Families*; *Report 6: Disabled Children: Services, Transport and Education* (1989).
3. P. Sullivan, V. McCay and J. Scanlon, 'Sexual Abuse of Deaf Youth', *American Annals of the Deaf*, 3 (1987), pp. 256–62.
4. M. Kennedy, 'The Deaf Child who is Sexually Abused: Is there a Need for a Dual Specialism?', *Child Abuse Review*, 4: 2 (1990), pp. 3–6.
5. Allan Roeher Institute, *Vulnerable: Sexual Abuse and Children with Disabilities* (Ontario, 1988).
6. G. Hard and H. Plumb, 1987, cited in A. Craft, *Mental Handicap and Sexuality: Issues and Perspectives* (Kent-Costello Publishers, 1987).
7. H. Westcott, 'The Abuse of Disabled Children: A review of literature', *Child: Care, Health and Development*, 17: 4 (1992), pp. 243–58.
8. J. Hubert, *Administering Drugs to Young People with Severe Learning Difficulties: Social Care Research Findings*, 18 (1992), Joseph Rowntree Memorial Trust.
9. R. Marchant, *Bridging the Gap: Child Protection Work with Children with Multiple Disabilities* (NSPCC, 1993).
10. Professor Christina Lyon, *Challenging Behaviour and Learning Disabilities: The Legal Framework* (Mental Health Foundation, forthcoming).

(Continued)

11. Department of Health, *The Children Act Guidance and Regulations*, vol. 6, *Children with Disabilities* (London, HMSO, 1991), section 15.4.

12. S. Brannan, *The Castle Hill School Report Practice Guide* (Shropshire County Council, 1993).

13. Allan Roeher Institute, *No More Victims: A Manual to Guide the Police in Addressing the Sexual Abuse of People with a Mental Handicap* (Ontario, 1992).

14. *Op. cit.* (n. 12).

15. Gulbenkian Foundation, *One Scandal Too Many* (Gulbenkian Foundation/Turnaround Distribution, 1993).